The Christian's Guide to Worry-free Money Management

The Christian's Guide to Worry-free Money Management

Daniel D. Busby, CPA
Kent E. Barber, CFP
Robert L. Temple, CIC, CFP

ZondervanPublishingHouse

Grand Rapids, Michigan

A Division of HarperCollinsPublishers

THE CHRISTIAN'S GUIDE TO WORRY-FREE
MONEY MANAGEMENT

Copyright © 1994 by Daniel D. Busby, Kent E. Barber,
Robert L. Temple

For information, write to
Zondervan Publishing House
5300 Patterson Avenue, S.E.
Grand Rapids, MI 49530

Library of Congress Cataloging-in-Publication Data

Busby, Daniel D., Barber, Kent E., Temple, Robert L.
    The Christian's guide to worry-free money manage-
ment / Daniel D. Busby, Kent E. Barber, Robert L.
Temple.
       p.   cm.
    ISBN 0-310-46231-2
       1. Finance, Personal—Religious aspects—Christianity.
I.Title.

Edited by Mary McCormick
Cover design by Mark Veldheer

This publication is intended to provide guidance in regard
to the subject matter covered. It is sold with the understanding that the authors and publisher are not herein
engaged in rendering legal, accounting, tax, financial
planning or other professional services. If such services
are required, professional assistance should be sought.

Printed in the United States of America

94 95 96 97 98 99 / DH / 10 9 8 7 6 5 4 3 2 1

Dedication

This book is dedicated to our six children, Julie and Alan Busby, Greg and Kim Barber, and Ashley and Julie Temple.

May God bless you on your journey as you apply the Scriptures and these money-management principles to the resources God entrusts to you.

"We will tell the next generation."
Psalm 78:4

Acknowledgments

To our wives, Claudette Busby, Jane Barber, and Melinda Temple: Thanks for your support and understanding as we worked on this project.

To our parents: Thanks for your example and guidance. We learned much of what we know from you.

To a host of individuals who reviewed our work: Thanks for your valuable suggestions.

Contents...

There are over 2,300 references to money and possessions in the Bible. In comparison, prayer is mentioned over 500 times. Prayer is key to successful Christian living. It is the very lifeline that keeps us connected with our heavenly Father. But His concern for our financial well-being is also quite obvious. His eternal wisdom saw the economic pitfalls of our lives even before time began. He wants the best for us.

"'I know the plans I have for you,' declares the Lord, 'plans to prosper you and not to harm you, plans to give you hope and a future.'"
·················· *Jeremiah 29:11* ··················

But how do we practice the principles of financial well-being that God has outlined in Scripture?
- Are we depending on Him if we plan ahead and invest money for the future?
- Are we to only use ultra-conservative investments like insured certificates of deposit?
- If it is ultimately God's money, how much of a risk should we take with it?
- Is investing in the stock market a gamble?
- Does purchasing insurance demonstrate a lack of faith in God?

Many Christians haven't come to an agreement about these vital questions. No wonder money management sometimes seems difficult and confusing.

Once our relationship with God is established, it is easier for us to follow His plan for worry-free money management. We will discover that our money actually belongs to Him. He loans it to us for our use as steward-managers, and naturally we will give much of it back to Him. In return, God has promised to supply all of our needs.

"My God will meet all your needs according to his glorious riches in Christ Jesus."
················· *Philippians 4:19* ···············

Many Christians fear that there will be a financial collapse. Some are so consumed by that fear that it leads to financial paralysis.

"Hope ties us to the future just as memory ties us to the past."

Could a total collapse come? Possibly—not probably. But fear of the future—financial or otherwise—is not God's plan for the Christian. Jesus advised,

> *"Do not let your hearts be troubled. Trust in God; trust also in me."*
> •••••••••••••••••• *John 14:1* ••••••••••••••••

There will always be disruptions in the economy, job layoffs, health problems, accidents, and stock-market declines. But just as a child reaches for the hand of a father while crossing a busy and dangerous intersection, we can put our trust in the heavenly Father. Jesus said, "In this world you will have trouble. But take heart! I have overcome the world" (John 16:33).

This book will give you a balanced approach to worry-free money management.

- You can have financial freedom.
- There is hope for your financial future.
- You can live within the plan God has designed for you.

Have the authors always perfectly followed the principles discussed here? We wish we had! It took each of us half our lifetime to reach our present level of understanding. Our own experiences and the years spent helping others with their money have expanded our view.

The primary themes of this book?

- Depend on and trust in God.
- Handle money responsibly.
- Give generously.
- Save mightily.
- Work industriously.
- Invest wisely.

If you have failed in your handling of money, try again. There is hope! It's never too late! You can manage your money worry-free.

Daniel D. Busby
Kent E. Barber
Robert L. Temple

"Fear is the darkroom where negatives are developed."

*"Put this money
to work," he said,
"until I come back."
Luke 19:13*

God's Plan for
Money Management

▶ It All Belongs to God

▶ Don't Worry About Money

▶ Understand God's Work Ethic

▶ Develop a Lifestyle of Giving

▶ Seek Good Counsel

▶ Save, Spend, and Invest Wisely

▶ Taxes Are Your Responsibility

▶ Use Debt Cautiously

▶ Take a Long-Term View

In God's plan, money is simply a medium of exchange. Money is temporal (earthly) and will ultimately pass away.

"Do not store up for yourselves treasures on earth, where moth and rust destroy, and where thieves break in and steal. But store up for yourselves treasures in heaven, where moth and rust do not destroy, and where thieves do not break in and steal. For where your treasure is, there your heart will be also" (Matthew 6:19-21).

As part of God's creation, we are to use money wisely. Our focus must always be on things that are eternal and not only the things of earth—on the Creator instead of His creation. How we use money is a reflection of our trust in Him and obedience to His word.

A clear understanding of God's principles about money will be life-changing.

"Get all you can.
Save all you can.
Give all you can!"
John Wesley

It All Belongs to God

Your attitude about money will affect all your decisions about what you do with it. As a Christian, your attitude should be that of a steward-manager, not as an owner. All the money and possessions we have actually belong to the Lord.

"The earth is the Lord's, and everything in it, the world, and all who live in it" (Psalm 24:1).

Stewardship implies certain responsibilities that ownership does not. Ownership suggests complete independence of authority and accountability. As a steward-manager, you are accountable for the way you use the assets God has given you. You are not free to act irresponsibly or without accountability.

"It is required that those who have been given a trust must prove faithful" (1 Corinthians 4:2).

It is not only important how you spend your money during your lifetime, it is also important to make provisions for its wise use after your death. Your stewardship responsibility will affect

Happy is the person who has learned to hold the things of this world with a loose hand.

future generations.

There's an old story of a young man who was given an assignment to build a house for his boss. He was instructed to spare no expense in workmanship and materials. Knowing the boss would be away during the entire project, the builder decided to cut corners—physically and materially. Much to his surprise, when the boss returned he made the generous announcement that the house was actually a gift to the builder. Now the young man had to live in the house made with poor workmanship and materials.

In building your financial house, remember that unwise building will not only affect you but also those who come after you. Your responsibility to provide for your family does not end when your life ends.

"If anyone does not provide for his relatives, and especially for his immediate family, he has denied the faith" (1 Timothy 5:8).

The world may continue beyond our lives. Even the apostles of the New Testament were looking for Christ's imminent return following His death, burial, and resurrection.

We must learn to balance the imperatives. On the one hand, we are to anticipate the Second Coming of the Lord Jesus Christ. On the other, He told us to "occupy" until He comes. In other words, we are to be diligent in faith and duty.

Many Christians plan as though Christ's coming will "rescue them" from the meager retirement benefits they will have due to their lack of savings and planning. They live only for the present rather than preparing for the future.

Their lack of savings is most often the result of unwise spending without thought of future benefits, not the result of extra giving. The scriptural admonition to "take no thought for the future" refers to worry, not planning.

Don't Worry About Money

"**W**orry" comes from a root word that means to strangle. The dictionary implies then that worrying is strangling oneself with disturbing thoughts.

Francis Ellis tells about a businessman who drew up a "worry chart." He discovered that 40% of his worries were about things that would never happen; 30% involved past decisions that couldn't be undone; 12% were about the opinions of others; and 10% were concerns about his health. He concluded that only 8% of his worries were legitimate.

Worry is paralyzing, and Christians are advised not to get caught in its stranglehold:

"Do not worry about your life, what you will eat or drink; or about your body, what you will wear" (Matthew 6:25).

"Seek first his kingdom and his righteousness, and all these things will be given to you as well. Therefore do not worry about tomorrow . . ." (Matthew 6:33-34).

Since God owns it all, and we are simply steward-managers of what He has provided, then our responsibility is to trust and obey. Worry is neither trust nor obedience. God has promised to care and to provide for His own.

As steward-managers, we are to act with wisdom and responsibility. We live faithfully within God's perfect plan and use tools and information that He has provided. Biblical interpretations will allow a different style of money management for some than for others. But for each one, the important principle is that money is a medium of exchange, not an end in itself.

God has called us to spend our lives in a loving relationship serving Him and sharing the Good News of the gospel with a lost world. Fear of the future is a great hindrance in doing God's work.

Thank God we can be free from the slavery of worry!

Worry is like a rocking chair; it will give you something to do, but it won't get you anywhere.

Understand God's Work Ethic

Working is God's plan for our lives.

"Six days you shall labor and do all your work" (Exodus 20:9).

Using our talent in our chosen vocation is important to God. Jesus modeled it in His own life, "As long as it is day, we must do the work of him who sent me . . ." (John 9:4). As a child in the temple, He reminded His own family that He had to be busy doing His Father's business.

Idle hands were condemned in Bible times. The apostle Paul advised New Testament Christians, ". . . we gave you this rule: If a man will not work, he shall not eat" (2 Thessalonians 3:10).

It is said that the philosopher John Dewey heard a commotion from the upstairs of his house and ran up the stairway to discover that the bathtub had overflowed. There, his son stood bewildered as Dewey began to ponder how the overflow had ever happened. "Dad," he said, "This is not the time to philosophize. It is time to mop!"

There is a time to plan and there is a "time to mop." Income and provision for our family is the reward for working. The same apostle advised the Christians in Colosse, "Whatever you do, work at it with all your heart, as working for the Lord, not for men, since you know that you will receive an inheritance from the Lord as a reward" (Colossians 3:23, 24).

Of course, work is not always possible. Old age or disability will make many of us dependent upon the care and the abilities of others. But remember: God is a faithful provider—charity is not.

It is important to plan for a time when it may not be possible for you to work. You will then need to depend on what you have saved and invested to provide the necessary income.

"Work and play are words used to describe the same thing under differing conditions."
Mark Twain

6

Develop a Lifestyle of Giving

Christian giving begins with self. "I urge you, brothers, in view of God's mercy, to offer your bodies as living sacrifices, holy and pleasing to God . . ." (Romans 12:1). Bible history records that the New Testament Christians of Macedonia, "gave themselves first to the Lord" (2 Corinthians 8:5).

Giving is a fundamental law of God—as real as the law of gravity. God blesses those who give: "Give, and it will be given to you. A good measure, pressed down, shaken together and running over, will be poured into your lap. For with the measure you use, it will be measured to you" (Luke 6:38).

Giving is like priming a pump. It creates a perpetual motion of supply. Christians don't just give to receive a supply, however. Christians give in obedience to the Word of God.

Christian stewardship makes us partners with God. The highest motive for giving is as an expression of love for our Lord. Giving to our church and other Christian charities helps those ministries pay their bills. But, more important, it does something for us spiritually. It enlarges our vision for ministry, develops character, and enriches our lives.

Our knowledge of fractions may be limited, but God in His wisdom gave the simplest method possible for computing the tithe. Whether we are figuring on a large or small amount, the simplest among us can move a decimal point to the left one position, and there it is—the tithe.

Tithing is a very practical biblical principle (see Malachi 3:10). It is simply giving a tenth of all our earnings back to God. The Old Testament advice, "Honor the Lord with your wealth, with the firstfruits of all your crops" (Proverbs 3:9), is complemented by Jesus' reminder in the New Testament, "You give God a tenth . . . but you neglect justice and the love of God. You should have practiced the latter without leaving the former undone" (Luke 11:42).

Jesus advised the combination of meeting the

First give yourself to God, then giving your possessions will be easy and joyful.

God's Attitude Toward Money and Wealth

Principle	Scripture Reference
1. God owns it all • We are stewards, not owners • Faithfulness in the use of money is basic to receiving God's blessing	Luke 19:13-27 Matthew 25:14-30 Romans 14:12 Luke 16:1-13
2. God's blessings make us rich • God rewards those who give	Proverbs 10:22 Ecclesiastes 5:19 Malachi 3:10
3. The love of money is wrong	Luke 12:15 1 Timothy 6:10
4. You cannot serve both God and money	Matthew 6:24
5. We are responsible for what God has provided	Luke 12:47, 48 Luke 19:15

God Instructs us to DO These Things

Principle	Scripture Reference
1. Depend on God	Philippians 4:19 John 14:1
2. Keep your promises • Debts must be paid	Ecclesiastes 5:4, 5 Psalm 37:21
3. Pay your taxes • Must know and obey the laws	Luke 20:22-25 Romans 13:7
4. Be reasonable • Be content • Have a moderate standard of living	1 Timothy 6:6-8 Hebrews 13:5
5. Be faithful even in small things	Matthew 25:23-30
6. Make plans • Be wise	Luke 14:28-30 Proverbs 21:5 Proverbs 24:3, 4
7. Giving is important • Tithing • Give out of love • Give cheerfully Give bountifully and you will reap bountifully • Giving stores up treasures in heaven	1 Corinthians 16:2 Proverbs 3:9, 10 Deuteronomy 26:1, 2 10, 11 Malachi 3:10 1 Timothy 6:18, 19 2 Corinthians 9:6-11 Matthew 6:19-21 Luke 11:42

God Instructs us to DO These Things *continued*

		Scripture Reference
8.	Expect to receive as a result of giving	Luke 6:38 Malachi 3:10,11
9.	Obtain good counsel • Ask for wisdom and understanding	Proverbs 15:22 Proverbs 14:15 Proverbs 13:20 James 1:5
10.	Investing is better than protecting against loss • Poor investing reaps punishment • Count the cost and evaluate an investment	Matthew 25:23-30 Luke 14:28
11.	Provide for your family	1 Timothy 5:8
12.	Parents are to teach their children	Proverbs 22:6 Psalm 78:4
13.	A good man leaves an inheritance for future generations	Proverbs 13:22
14.	Working is God's plan	Colossians 3:23, 24

God Instructs us to AVOID AND NOT DO These Things

	Principle	Scripture Reference
1.	Avoid pride	1 Timothy 6:17
2.	Avoid greed	1 Timothy 6:9, 10 Luke 12:15
3.	Avoid hoarding money	James 5:3
4.	Do not be anxious about the future • Do not worry	Matthew 6:25-34
5.	Do not try to get rich quick	Proverbs 28:20 Proverbs 13:11
6.	Do not co-sign for another • Borrow with caution	Proverbs 22:26, 27 Proverbs 22:7 Proverbs 11:15
7.	Do not love money	Matthew 6:21, 24
8.	Do not rely on the uncertainty of riches	1 Timothy 6:17-19

The rewards of giving in this life are good. But the rewards in the next life are infinitely better.

A lifestyle of generous giving is God's plan for you.

standards of righteous living with the paying of the tithe in His conversation with the teachers and Pharisees of New Testament times (see Matthew 23:23).

Liberal giving beyond the tithe is determined by God's leading in the life of the individual Christian. The Bible indicates that giving "above and beyond" has its own reward, "Whoever sows generously will also reap generously . . . Each man should give what he has decided in his heart to give, not reluctantly or under compulsion, for God loves a cheerful giver" (2 Corinthians 9:6, 7).

God promises generous givers an increase in their possessions. "You will be made rich in every way," Paul says, "so that you can be generous on every occasion, and . . . your generosity will result in thanksgiving to God" (2 Corinthians 9:11). Paul isn't saying that God is going to make us rich. He says that if we are generous, God will enable us to be even more generous.

Money is necessary to advance God's kingdom. Pastors, missionaries, and other church workers are supported by the money brought to the "storehouse" (the church). Giving is God's plan for your entire lifetime and through your estate.

Seek Good Counsel

A 16-year-old named William left home to seek his fortune. His earthly possessions were tied in a bundle carried in his hand. One day he met an elderly canal-boat captain who listened to his story of how his family was too poor to keep him and that the only skill he had was making candles and soap.

The old captain knelt and prayed for the boy's future, and, afterward gave him some advice. "William, someone will be the leading soap-maker in New York. It could be you. Be a good man, give your heart to Christ, pay the Lord all that belongs to Him, make an honest soap, give a full pound, and I'm certain you'll be a prosperous and rich man." The 16-year-old who listened to godly counsel was William Colgate, who not only prospered beyond his wildest dreams but was also able to give millions to the Lord's cause.

The trusted counsel of those who are wise in money matters is very important. "Plans fail for lack of counsel, but with many advisers they succeed" (Proverbs 15:22). Christians should seek out those who have wisdom and understanding in money matters for counseling in money management.

Wise counsel will often come from another Christian. But don't fall into the trap of thinking that Christians are always your best source for advice. They aren't.

Above all, you may rest in the assurance of God's promise, "If any of you lacks wisdom, he should ask God, who gives generously to all without finding fault, and it will be given to him" (James 1:5).

"Good counselors lack no clients."
Shakespeare

Save, Spend, and Invest Wisely

Tennyson, in "Idylls of the King," gives the knight's pledge: "Live pure, speak truth, right the wrong, follow the king." That pledge may also describe a Christian lifestyle. As we have seen, God has promised us heavenly wisdom for living here on planet earth. He has also gifted us with common sense and the ability to discern between right and wrong.

Jesus promised a spiritual advantage in the Person of the Holy Spirit, who indwells the believer. "The Counselor, the Holy Spirit, whom the Father will send in my name, will teach you all things . . ." (John 14:26).

Spirit-led logic calls us to live a life uniquely separate from the attitude and actions of the world. A lifestyle that satisfies the lust of the eyes or boasts of what one has and does is not acceptable to God (1 John 2:15-17). "Piling up" money beyond reason or a consumptive lifestyle are forbidden just as clearly as adultery.

A Christian should also seek to live within his or her means. That takes practice and discipline. The apostle cautioned, "I have learned to be content whatever the circumstances" (Philippians 4:11). For some, driving a luxury car is living within their means. Others may be more "content" driving a compact. Each has a responsibility to be a wise steward-manager of God's resources and *live moderately.*

God's Word gives us understanding about the source of material blessings, "Every good and perfect gift is from above, coming down from the Father . . ." (James 1:17). Using those blessings wisely is key to good stewardship.

Saving is setting aside a portion of your earnings on a regular basis. It involves spending less in the short-term and investing for long-term benefits. Those benefits may include a vacation, automobile, or a down payment on that "dream home."

What you do to earn money on your savings is called "investing" (short-term or long-term). The goal is balancing the risk of not investing with the risk of investing in the wrong thing (and possibly losing the investment). Gain comes from interest that is added to the principal. This, in turn, earns interest.

Gain may also come from the increased value of principal or investments (such as equity investments in stocks or real estate).

Planning for the future recognizes your responsibility for managing the resources at your disposal and helps you fulfill your duty as God's steward-manager. Your level of planning will determine the quality of your life—and that of your family—during your retirement years.

Saving, investing, and spending wisely doesn't guarantee carefree living in later years. However, failure to save will reduce your options (whether or not you will need to work). Increased physical limitations may prevent you from working, even though you may need the income.

God's providing and our planning go hand in hand. "The man who plants and the man who waters have one purpose, and each will be rewarded according to his own labor. For we are God's fellow workers" (1 Corinthians 3:8, 9).

Taxes Are Your Responsibility

Jesus was asked, "Is it right for us to pay taxes to Caesar or not?" He answered: "Give to Caesar what is Caesar's, and to God what is God's" (Luke 20:22-25).

Christians are citizens of two worlds, earth and heaven. As citizens of earth, there are certain responsibilities that cannot be abandoned. The apostle Paul advised the Christians of Rome,

"*Everyone must* submit himself to the governing authorities, for there is no authority except that which God has established . . ." (Romans 13:1, italics added).

Christians must know and obey tax laws—even if our taxes support abortion clinics. Remember, Rome did far worse with their taxes.

The law does not mandate that you pay the most tax possible, it simply gives the "rules of the game." If you've ever played a board game, you know that there are certain rules that you must know and apply if you are going to play fairly and attempt to win the game. Likewise, there are "rules" for using strategies that may minimize the taxes that are paid.

These are perfectly legal, and as Christians, knowing and using them are important in being a good steward-manager. Though tax laws impact your life from the day you are born until the day you die, your responsibility is to preserve as much as possible from unnecessary tax loss.

Income- and estate-tax laws constantly change, and what you don't know about the "rules of the game" may cost you and your estate a fortune in taxes.

Use Debt Cautiously

You may be one of the millions of Christians who have credit cards, or have borrowed money to buy a home, car, or furniture. Are you violating a biblical standard? No. The Bible neither prohibits borrowing nor promotes debt.

Paul advised the Christians of Rome, "Let no debt remain outstanding, except the continuing debt to love one another" (Romans 13:8). Faithfulness in paying debt is one of the marks of a Christian lifestyle.

Every effort should be made to repay debt. The Scriptures warn, "The wicked borrow and do not repay . . ." (Psalm 37:21). Even if you are meeting all your payments, is the debt load so heavy that it negatively affects your life and your family? Have you become a slave to debt? That is definitely not God's plan for the Christian.

"Jesus said, 'If you hold to my teaching, you are really my disciples. Then you will know the truth, and the truth will set you free'" (John 8:31-32).

Heavy indebtedness is caused by presuming on your future ability to pay an obligation. You may be falling into the debt trap by buying a home or driving an automobile that you cannot afford.

The amount of debt a person can adequately handle varies from one individual to another. Because of limited finances, some may not be able to positively handle ANY debt. There are

Credit-Card Warning!
• • • • • • • • • • • • • • •

Use of credit cards may encourage overspending. Often a purchase will be made more readily by using a credit card than if paying by cash or a check. Buying a "sale" item on your credit card is no bargain if your credit card bill is paid off in installments with interest. If you find yourself doing this, you need to learn the discipline by going without credit cards.

some important cautions in using debt.

- **Co-signing on loans.** The Bible counsels the Christian about providing surety or co-signing on a loan for another, "A man lacking in judgment strikes hands in pledge and puts up security for his neighbor" (Proverbs 17:18).

- **Bankruptcy.** Voluntary bankruptcy should be taken only as a last recourse and then only to protect your creditors. Avoiding repayment of your obligations through bankruptcy is not an acceptable option.

- **Use of credit cards.** Credit-card debt should be avoided because of the high interest rates. Credit-card interest rates are almost always higher than what you can reasonably expect to earn after paying taxes on a very good investment.

Overextended credit-card balances usually cause the greatest heartache for the Christian family. Using credit cards and paying the balance in full is different from avoiding credit-card debt. Using them for convenience and recordkeeping may even be a good money-management practice.

The key to worry-free money management is learning good spending habits. Money can be used to honor God in every part of your life. Learn to control your spending. Paying high interest rates on past spending is not God's plan. Depending on Him to pay for what you consumed yesterday is wrong. Depending on Him for income to pay for today's needs and future needs is the sign of a good steward-manager.

Being debt-free is a worthy goal, and accomplishing it will give you greater freedom to serve the Lord. Many have even found a greater freedom to give beyond the tithe. If you have a concern about the debts you owe, giving beyond the tithe becomes more difficult for you. For most people, being debt-free is a goal not yet realized.

It is reasonable to have your home paid for before you retire. If you can accomplish this before retirement, you will have more to give to the Lord's work and save toward your retirement needs.

"Whatever lies behind us and what lies before us, are tiny matters compared to what lies within us."
Holmes

*Little and often
make much.*

Take a Long-Term View

D. L. Moody, the Chicago shoe salesman who became a world-renowned evangelist, is said to have given this advice to his sons on his deathbed, "If God be your partner, make your plans large." Partnership with God includes a lifetime of service— whether it is the giving of our lives or our resources. He expects a long-term pattern of consistency.

The same principle applies to our money management. It is the steady, consistent approach that pays huge dividends. If you only have a short-term view of your investments, you will likely jump out of your mutual fund every time the Dow-Jones drops 100 points. You may also have your money parked on the sidelines when the market turns upward.

One of the primary advantages of taking the long-term view is harnessing the power of time. As several small streams make a mighty river, your modest but steady saving and investing over a longer period allows your money to grow and "compound."

If your money is placed inside a tax-deferred vehicle like an IRA or 401(k) plan, the power of compounding multiplies because taxes are not paid until the money is withdrawn from the account.

Taking the long-term view will protect you from putting your money into some get-rich-quick scheme. You may be tempted by a friend telling you about a new investment where you can receive 100% return on your money in a year, for example. "Not many people know about the opportunity yet, and you can get in on the ground floor!" But with the long-term view, you are more likely to keep your focus on your goals. It's a proven principle: If the investment is too good to be true, it probably *is* just that.

Get your destination in sight. Then start early, save mightily and regularly. Hit singles on a regular basis with your money over the long-term. Leave the home runs to those who can risk striking out. It worked for Ty Cobb—it will work for you.

Study Guide Questions

1. Explain the difference between stewardship and ownership.

2. How can we find a financial balance between occupying until He comes and anticipating His second coming?

3. How can you avoid worrying about your financial future?

4. What does the Bible teach about work?

5. Why is generous giving important?

6. What type of financial counsel should you seek?

7. What is the meaning of wise saving, spending, and investing?

8. What is the scriptural view toward paying taxes?

9. What are the biblical standards about assuming debt?

10. Why should you develop a long-term view towards money management?

Step 2

Money and Your Family

"For I have learned to be content whatever the circumstances. I know what it is to be in need, and I know what it is to have plenty. I have learned the secret of being content in any and every situation . . ."
Philippians 4:11, 12

▶ Mixing Love and Money

▶ Raising Money-Smart Kids

▶ Strategies for Your Home Ownership

▶ Buying or Leasing Your Car

▶ Planning Early to Meet College Expenses

▶ Slow and Steady Ways to Build Cash

▶ Avoiding Financial-Planning Mistakes

Families make finances complicated. Ask any new parent who is suddenly talking about funding a college education. Ask any newlywed who is busy changing the beneficiaries on her company retirement plan. Or ask anybody who has just realized that his aging parents are no longer able to care for themselves. When you get right down to it, personal finance revolves pretty much around the family.

Traditionally, family financial planning meant taking on house payments and raising children in your 20s and 30s, sending the kids to college when you were in your 40s, building wealth in your 50s, and focusing on estate planning and grandchildren in your 60s.

But with many people delaying marriage and children, and with the rise of second marriages and second families, the traditional rules often do not apply. These days, families may have to deal with both toddlers and aging parents at the same time. Or they may be funding their kids' education just as they begin retirement.

Today's financial planning decisions are influenced less by your age than the ages of your children and your parents. The only thing dependent on your age is retirement planning.

Still, the basic rules don't change. Families need to balance current lifestyle against future needs such as a house down payment, college tuition, or retirement. In addition, at each life stage, family members have to consider four things—giving, investing, insurance, and what they will leave behind.

Taking a long-term view is essential. Today's decisions may impact future resources. Your short-term financial decisions also have long-term spiritual implications. "Seek first his kingdom and his righteousness, and all these things will be given to you as well" (Matthew 6:33). Temporal (earthly) choices should be made with eternity in mind. As dual citizens of heaven and earth, Christians have an obligation to invest in the concerns of the Kingdom as well as their own.

"The eyes of other people are the eyes that ruin us. If all but myself were blind, I should want neither fine clothes, fine houses, nor fine furniture."
Benjamin Franklin

Mixing Love and Money

"There are two ways to have enough money: One is to continue to accumulate more. The other is to desire less."
G.K. Chesterton

No doubt about it—your kids will get a financial education just by watching and listening to mom and dad. How you and your spouse work out family finances will have a large impact on your kids' attitude toward money. Despite the influence of TV and their peers, it's likely they'll end up the spitting image of you. This is just one reason to work out a mutually agreeable approach to handling money in your family.

There must be a commitment by a husband and a wife to have unity about family finances. It will be a commitment to reconcile differing priorities and agree upon common goals. Unless both individuals have a personal relationship with Jesus Christ, unity about money will be very difficult to achieve.

Start with the checkbook. Start by figuring out who is going to balance the checkbook. Does one of you enjoy adding up numbers while the other can't be bothered with such details?

There's nothing wrong with his and her checking accounts. But a joint account will make things a lot easier when it comes to paying household bills, and it could help to cement your marriage.

Recognize your differing financial "styles." Examine your basic attitudes toward finances. Each of you probably came from homes with differing financial styles—conflict of these styles is normal. Even when two hearts beat as one, some of these contrasting money-styles will often be encountered:

- Do you scold or make your spouse feel guilty for spending too much money—and are you chided in return for being too stingy?
- Within your family, are you reluctant to talk about money or do you share about it freely?
- Do you prefer to operate on a budget but your spouse likes to operate "out-of-pocket"?
- Your spouse wants lots of extra money in the checking account but you want to invest.

None of the money personalities described above

is necessarily bad. As the old one-liner goes, "Show me a couple that doesn't disagree about money, and I'll show you a couple on the way to their wedding." What you need to do is keep from getting too far out of balance—meet your partner halfway.

Develop a "debt strategy." You or your spouse may have accumulated credit-card debt, a car loan, or a college loan before your marriage. So instead of a decision on whether to incur debt, you must initially figure out what to do with the debt you already have.

It is common for men to have a greater tolerance for debt than women. This is because men tend to see money as a flow that just keeps on coming, while many women see it as a pool that can be drained empty.

Regardless of the perception of debt by each spouse, excessive debt can have a devastating effect on your spiritual life and the marriage relationship. Uncontrolled family debt may force you to work two jobs. You may be unable to grasp vocational opportunities because of the lack of freedom due to debt. (See Step 4 for more reasons to keep a healthy respect for debt.)

Has one spouse learned to save for major purchases and the other one wants to buy everything on credit? Early in your marriage, develop your debt strategy. Agree to avoid borrowing for consumption (credit card debt and vacations). Borrow only for long-term debt (a home, education, or investment property) and, even then, use caution.

Find your financial balance. *First,* get an objective opinion from an expert. Few couples can afford to hire a financial counselor, but a number of good books at your local library are excellent sources of expert advice. Take a look as well at current financial magazines and financial-advice columns in other periodicals. This is the best way to get beyond "your way versus my way" to a genuinely better solution.

Second, ask your parents if the approaches they took—and the ones you learned by example—genuinely worked well. You may be surprised to find that they disagreed over a particular strategy and had to come to an agreeable solution.

With a little honesty, flexibility, and discipline, you and your spouse can find a reasonable, workable, and mutually acceptable strategy for managing your money—*then it won't manage you.*

Raising Money-Smart Kids

All parents want their children to grow up to become responsible, independent adults. If you gradually teach your children how to handle money appropriately, they will be ready for the demands of the adult world.

Surveys show that less than 40% of parents talk about money with their children. So where do kids learn money management? They learn from advertising and from watching their parents. When they become adults, most of them will follow your example in money management.

When to start teaching about money. Like brushing teeth, financial responsibility is a habit that is easiest to establish when children are young. But teaching kids about money is a long-term project that can take a lot of parental time and patience.

Teaching your children the stewardship of God's resources is essential. But you need to get a jump-start on the media. Children are being influenced by TV, movies, and advertisements. They get an over-glamorous view of credit cards. They think they can get more than they can pay for.

You can't just sit down and say, "Now I am going to teach you about money." You have to bring it down to their level.

Children and ATMs • • • • • • • • • • • • • • •

The next time you take your children with you to get cash out of an automatic teller machine, take the time to explain how the money got there—that it had to be earned. It is a disservice to children to make them think getting cash out of a machine is magical fun and you can do it anytime you need it.

Teach by example. The way you handle your own money will make a stronger statement to your child than anything you say. Christian stewardship principles will be clearly taught if you model proper values and attitudes toward money.

Be honest with your kids. If you are known to have the first dollar you ever made, tell the kids you have a tendency to pinch pennies. Tell them whether you consider it a good—or bad—trait. If you struggle to stay within a budget, share that information. They'll figure it out anyway.

What is the basis of paying an allowance? Family membership alone should be the basis for an allowance.

Avoid Surprises with Children • • • • • • • • • • • • •

You should tell children early on if the only way you can afford Harvard or Yale is if they get a scholarship. Or make it clear that they'll have to earn money to help pay their college living expenses. They may not like these discussions. But if you wait until later and then bring it up, they will probably like it less.

When to start paying an allowance. When your child begins to express needs at the grocery check-out counter, it's time to start a weekly allowance. By age 3, most children are aware of the relationship between money and shopping. Once you start paying an allowance, pay them regularly, on time, and without having to be reminded. Provide the money in a variety of small-denomination coins and bills. For example, a $1.00 allowance could be given in two quarters, three dimes, two nickels and ten pennies.

How to determine the amount of the allowance. Provide enough allowance to cover giving, spending, and saving. The spending portion can be used however the child pleases but do not encourage wastefulness.

For preschoolers, set up a system of banks: one each for giving, spending, and saving. Explain their purpose. The *giving* bank is money set aside for our tithe to God. The *spending* bank is for everyday spending money. The *saving* bank is money that stays in the bank and accumulates until you

"Kids who have everything soon lose respect for money and for their parents." Ann Landers

need it for something special.

A recent national survey conducted by *Youth Monitor* reflected the following average weekly allowances:

Age	Amount
6 - 8	$1.99
9 - 11	4.17
12 - 13	5.82
14 - 15	9.68
16 - 17	10.80

Teach the principles of tithing. Teach your child to give 10% of their allowance and earnings to God, through your church.

Teach the principles of saving. Give your child reasons to save. The younger the child, the smaller and more immediate the goal should be; it ought to be something—a toy truck, a doll—that the child can reach within a few weeks. As he gets older, it may be a fancy bike. Regardless of the age, teaching the child to work and save for a goal is what's important.

Set guidelines on how much money can be used out of savings for short-term goals versus longer-term goals like a college education. Most families allow children to withdraw a certain portion of their savings.

How not to use an allowance. An allowance is not a substitute for your time or your love. *Allowances should never depend on the child's behavior or good grades.* But a *bonus* for A's and B's may be motivating for some children.

How to provide money in addition to the allowance. Tie additional payments to extra chores like raking leaves or washing the car. Pay them as soon as the job is done. This teaches your child that money relates to work.

Teaching Christian values about money. You will have many opportunities to teach your child about how a Christian deals with money. How you handle experiences like these will teach your child volumes about what is right and wrong:

• **ATM machines.** What if you request a $50 withdrawal but the machine gives you $100 but only charges you for $50? Do you contact the bank and return the extra money?

- **Store checker.** You are buying an item at the store and the checker charges you $2 for something that costs $5. Do you call it to the checker's attention?
- **Finding a lost item.** You find a billfold that contains $200 and the owner's name and address. Do you return the billfold and the money to the owner?
- **Admission based on age.** Your child is small for their age. You are paying for your family's admission to the fun park and the admission is based on the children's age. Do you pay the proper admission price?

Talking to your children about these situations as they occur will help them make the right decisions when they are on their own.

When it's time to open a bank account. Open a bank account for your child when they have saved enough money. You may have to co-sign the account. Be sure the bank waives the service charge for kids.

Money and Teens

Budgeting is difficult for teens. Focus instead on a "spending plan" based on their interests and activities. It will seem less constraining than a budget.

Teach children the value of work. By the time they are age 13 or 14, they should be earning enough money that you can eliminate their allowance. By that time, their rewards should be internal; if your son does a good job of cleaning up the garage,

Teens Can Manage Money

Provide the learning experiences they need:
- **Personal checking account.** Balanced under your supervision.
- **Personal budget.** Made useful by simple recordkeeping, planning, and evaluation.
- **Exposure to investments.** Savings account, collectibles, securities—even a real estate investment in partnership with you. Attend an investment seminar together.
- **Credit card.** Should you help your teen get a credit card? Generally, no. There is plenty of time for them to get their own card when they are out of high school or college!

compliment her effort and comment on the satisfaction he must feel.

Where will they get their money? They may be working for you or working outside the home—but their money should come from work. This approach will provide them with invaluable insights into money management.

If you do your job of modeling Christian stewardship values, the world of finance and economics with its pitfalls and opportunities will be no mystery to your children. They will become adults knowing not only how to make a living—but even more important—how to **live**.

Communicate with teens openly about your family's financial position—especially regarding college—while your teen is in junior high school. If you can afford only a state school, say so. That gives them time to earn money or boost their grades to get more financial aid if they want to go somewhere else.

Talking to Adult Children About Money

Keep adult children informed about your estate planning, so they can make their own plans. For example, you don't want them waiting around for an inheritance that may not exist. Surprising kids by your estate plan can cause great family heartache.

Such family financial conversations are never easy, but they are almost always harder for the children to initiate. When the kids have to take the initiative, they may be viewed as being greedy or grasping. When the parents take the initiative, all those psychological concerns can be dissipated.

Investment-Smart Tip for Your Children

Buy a stock certificate for your child. The minimum fee at most brokers is $20 to $50. Try a discount stock broker (see page 163 for a list of these brokers). They may charge as little as 16% of the stock's price—or $6.56 for $41 Disney.

Strategies for Home Ownership

A young couple told friends that they were on solid financial ground in buying a new home. "How do you know?" the friend asked. "Because," they answered in virtual unison, "our realtor said we could afford a house that was three times our income."

The friend responded, "Oh," and shifted to another topic, not wanting to question their realtor's authority nor pop their balloon of joy. There is nothing like a good ratio—no matter how meaningless—to make a sale!

A home may be the most significant investment you will make during your lifetime. After you are sure of God's direction on the purchase of your first house or a move up in your housing, apply the following concepts to be the best steward of God's resources.

Location. Identify the differences between your needs and your wants. Your parents probably worked for many years to finally have the house of their dreams. Don't expect your first, second, or even your third home to equal the home you remember in your high school or college years.

With investments, the watchword is *diversify, diversify, diversify.* In real estate, the guiding principle is *location, location, location.* Location will probably have a dramatic effect on the price you will pay. To live in an area of your choice, you may need to accept a house with less square footage than you would otherwise prefer.

Don't think that home ownership is going to automatically be a no-brainer investment decision. Real

Tips for Home Buyers

- **Frequent house buying and selling doesn't make sense anymore.** With housing appreciation running at only 3% to 5% a year in most places, it may take seven years or more of home ownership before you turn a profit when selling.
- **You need to find out what comparable houses have recently sold for before making bids.** To get a bargain, you have to know one when you see it. And that means you first have to see a lot of homes.
- **Everything is negotiable.** Price is the most negotiable element of the home purchase. But you may get other concessions like a new roof, a paint job, new air conditioning, heating units, or all the minor repairs you request.

estate, particularly residential real estate, has generally been in a slump during the past 5-10 years. So, look carefully at the location before making that final decision.

Your housing budget. How much can you afford to spend on housing? *Principal, interest, taxes,* and *insurance* are the major items. Try to limit your housing costs to no more than 40% of your disposable income—your gross income less income and social security taxes and your tithe. You may have to stretch the percentage to 45% to 50% of your disposable income if you live in an area where housing costs are extremely high.

Most mortgage companies will look at the total cost of operating and maintaining a house in determining the maximum amount they will finance. Then, depending on the location of the house, a lender may approve a loan with a monthly payment that will not exceed 45% of your gross monthly income.

Example ●

Bill and Judy are buying their first home and want to know how much of a monthly payment they can comfortably handle. They have been married for two years and do not have any children. Here is their combined income:

Salary	$50,000
Less:	
Tithe (minimum)	5,000
Social Security	3,825
Federal and state income taxes	10,000
Net disposable income	$33,175
Recommended housing cost limit	40%
Available for housing costs:	
Annually	$13,270
Monthly	$ 1,106

They selected a 30-year, 7% mortgage (see **Step 4** on home mortgages). The monthly principal and interest payment is $665. Here are the expenses on their proposed home:

Monthly Expenses

Principal & interest	$665
Property taxes	75
Homeowners insurance	25
Telephone	30
Water and sewer	15
Electric and gas	125
Maintenance	30
Contingency fund (improvements, furniture and so on)	100
Estimated monthly housing Expenses	$1,065

They can probably afford this home because estimated housing expenses are $41 per month less than the 40% guideline.

If you are stretching your income to cover expenses for a house purchase, don't reduce your tithe to make up the difference. God will honor you if you continue to pay His tithe.

Improvements to Your Home Can Reduce Your Tax Bill

Improvements add to your tax basis in your house. When you sell your home, the higher your tax basis, the lower your taxable gain. Even if you defer gains on home sales, the smaller the gain you defer, the lower your ultimate tax bill. *Just be sure to do it correctly.*

Keep in mind that home improvements can save you taxes; home repairs generally provide no tax benefit. Home improvements are expenditures that: **(1)** add value to a residence; **(2)** prolong its useful life; or **(3)** adapt it to a new use. Improvements aren't limited to major projects like adding a room.

Many smaller outlays count as capital expenditures, such as adding bookshelves. If you attach an item to your house and the change improves it, the item's cost may be added to your basis. Be sure to keep the receipts until you sell the house.

Also, make repairs part of a larger improvement project. Why? While the repairs aren't usually deductible, the cost of repairs made as part of a larger improvement project can be added to your basis. For example, you might patch your walls when you add bookshelves or add new or improved electrical outlets.

Home improvement costs, plus acquisition costs, comprise the tax basis in your home. The higher the basis, the lower your taxable gains when you sell.

Another strategy: Postpone repair work until 90 days before selling your house and pay for the work within 30 days after sale. Such fix-up costs can be deducted from the sale proceeds if you postpone the gain from selling your home.

Selling Your Home

The rapid price appreciation that your house enjoyed in the 1980s is gone. But real-estate retains one timeless virtue: It's still the repository of sweet tax breaks. The obvious ones are deductions on federal returns for mortgage interest and property taxes. There are a bunch of other real-estate maneuvers to reduce the Internal Revenue Service's take.

The most important one is figuring out the taxable profit from selling your house. Selling fees and home improvements can shrink the amount of profit you must report (see chart). Sorry, normal repairs, such as replacing a broken windowpane, don't count as improvements, which must boost the house's value (an extra room) or prolong its useful life (a new roof).

How to Save on Taxes From a Home • • • • • • • • • • • • • • • •

Buying a home for $50,000 in 1976 and selling it for $150,000 now doesn't have to mean a $100,000 taxable gain. Here's how:

$150,000	Selling price
- 10,000	Selling expenses*
- 90,000	Adjusted cost basis**
$ 50,000	Taxable profit

*Advertising, legal fees, agent's commission
**Original $50,000 price, plus $2,000 of closing costs in 1976 and $38,000 in home improvements

Beyond that, most people sidestep taxes altogether by rolling over the sales proceeds into buying the next home within two years. Trouble is, if after several houses you decide to become a renter, the accumulated profits from the previous homes are subject to taxes. That's why you should hold down the reportable profit, even if you roll over each time. The tax code does provide a bonus for sellers 55 and over: They can shield up to $125,000 in profits.

Did you lose money selling your residence? Too bad. That's not deductible. However, people who lose money on a sale of residential property which is converted to a rental are in better shape. They often can deduct some of that. They also get a break if they hang on to it and lose money because the rent falls short of mortgage and operating expenses.

Buying or Leasing Your Car

What's less fun than sticking your head into a barrel of hungry piranhas or having a root canal performed without anesthetic? Not much, actually, but buying or leasing a new car or truck probably ranks a close third, if not higher, on the pain index.

As a result, most people put more time, effort, and thought into buying a new sofa than purchasing or leasing a $15,000 vehicle. Expecting the worst, they delay the process until the last possible moment and then rush through it with reckless abandon. In so doing they often waste hundreds, or even thousands of dollars that could

Who Should Avoid Leasing
• • • • • • • • • • • • • • • • •

- **You want to save money.** The convenience and low payments of leasing have a price. You usually spend more, overall, leasing than buying.
- **You drive a lot.** If you drive more than 15,000 miles a year, your penalty may be 15 cents a mile for the extra miles.
- **You want to save money on insurance.** The temptation to get a more-expensive car when you lease than when you buy drives up insurance premiums.
- **You are not sure you will stay with the lease for the full term.** You will pay dearly to get out of the contract early.
- **You hate surprises.** Leases can be full of them: $500 to turn in the car at the end; a $400 "acquisition fee" to drive off in your new leased car.

There is probably not another ordinary consumer-transaction that matches leasing for complexity.

---

otherwise be recouped through careful preparation and clever negotiating.

Leases Bewitch and Bewilder

You've heard the pitches: $288 a month for a $20,077 Plymouth Grand Voyager minivan; $199 a month for a $15,525 Volkswagon Jetta III GL. Enticing? Yes. Cheap? Certainly, if compared with the payments when you buy a car. A bargain? Probably not. Confusing? Undoubtedly. Consumers are often so bedazzled by leasing's low monthly payments that they allow themselves to be overcharged on every other part of the complicated deal.

With all of the promotions for car leases, it's no wonder Americans are being drawn to leasing in record numbers. Currently, 24% of the new cars sold in the U.S. are leased. It is expected to rise to 40% by 1998.

The temptation is that a car lease allows you to drive a new, more expensive car at an affordable price. Leases require little down payment, usually just the first month's payment and a refundable security deposit equal to a monthly payment.

Since leases run for only a few years—typically two to three—you can always be driving a relatively new car. Maintenance should be minimal with a car that is in

---

Leasing-Smart Tips ...
• • • • • • • • • • • • • • •

- **Haggle on the price.** You can dicker on a lease just as you'd haggle over price if you were buying.
- **Understand the agreement.** You need to know the term of the lease, the capitalized cost (equivalent to the sales price), the residual (what the leasing company thinks the car will be worth at the end of the term), and the interest rate (or "money factor").
- **Consider your options.** You don't have to lease through a dealer. Banks, credit unions, and independent lease companies might have better deals.

your possession only a few years, and warranties often run the length of the lease.

Monthly payments are considerably less on a leased vehicle than on a vehicle that is bought with a conventional loan. When you pay for a car the conventional way, you contract to pay its entire cost over a specified period of time, typically two to five years. You pay back the entire amount financed, less any down payment, plus interest.

When you lease, you also make monthly payments for a specified time, and interest costs are factored in. But instead of paying back the entire cost of the vehicle, you pay only for what you use. Lease payments are based on the difference between the car's price new and the car's anticipated value—the residual—at the end of the lease. The residual is subtracted from the new price, then that number is divided evenly among the months in the contract.

> # Gap Insurance for Leases
> • • • • • • • • • • • • • • • • •
>
> If you have an accident a year into your lease, there'll likely be a big difference between what you'll have to pay the dealer and what the insurance company will pay you. Gap insurance doesn't cost very much—usually a couple of hundred dollars over the life of the lease.

A Jeep Grand Cherokee with a purchase price of $21,800 might cost $664 a month with a conventional three-year loan. The same vehicle, however, would cost half that amount—$318 a month over a three-year lease. The catch is that you would own the vehicle after three years under a purchase, but with most leases, you have no vehicle at the end of three years.

The auto industry likes leases because:
- Most leases are two or three years long, so you're back in the showroom often, generating more profits. Buyers, in contrast, go five years or more between purchases.
- Lease customers, expecially those who have two- or three-year leases, are likely to stay with the same dealer and brand.
- Leases can camouflage huge profits. Dealers sometimes mark up leased cars 10% or 20%

above the manufacturer's sticker without objection, because consumers are fixated on monthly payments.

Dealers aren't required to tell you the total cost of the car you're leasing. Compare that to credit cards, for instance, which have been required for years to plainly state their terms.

Companies aren't leasing cars for altruistic reasons. They are leasing because they make a lot of money off it.

The Traditional Car Purchase

If you want to drive your car more than two to three years, purchasing is usually better. If you buy a car and keep it for seven or eight years, you generally have less expensive transportation.

And if you want to actually own something after the term of the financing contract, you obviously want to buy rather than lease. The vehicle can be used as a trade-in on another vehicle.

The Buy-Versus-Lease Calculation • • • • • • • • • • • • • • • •

Consider using inexpensive software like *Expert Lease* from Chart Software (813-536-8093). By plugging in lease terms, you can calculate the finance rate—not usually revealed by dealers—as well as the difference in cash outlay versus traditional financing.

Here are some tips to help make your next car-buying experience a more pleasant experience:

Decide what type of vehicle will best suit your needs and budget. Narrow your choices and determine a target buying price you can reasonably afford. *Consumers Digest Buying Guide* can be a real help. Once you've decided on this figure, be prepared to stick to it steadfastly.

Call your insurance agent before you shop. Insuring a new vehicle can be a major expense in itself, depending on the type of car or truck you're buying, where you live, your age, sex, marital status, and driving record. Too often, people buy cars for which insurance premiums are equal to, or even higher than the car payments.

Select a dealer cautiously. If you live in or

Cheaper than leasing or buying a new car is buying a late-model used car.

---

near a big city, you'll probably have a choice of more than one dealer for a particular car line. Larger, high-volume dealers will usually have a better selection. Because they sell more vehicles than smaller dealers, they may be able to afford a smaller profit on each one they sell, which can make negotiating a bit easier.

Time your purchase wisely. While there is no single "best" time to shop for a new vehicle, there are some periods in which you may have a better negotiating edge. The end of the month is always a good time to buy, because dealers usually want to finish a month with strong sales, especially if they've had a slow start. Try not to purchase a new vehicle as soon as it hits the showrooms and is in big demand.

Arrange your financing carefully. You may be the one among many who can pay cash for your car. That's ideal. But if you are like most people, you need to finance the purchase. If so, give this aspect of the deal your strict attention to avoid losing money continuously over a four- or five-year term. Keep in mind that the finance and insurance department is a major profit center for any dealership, and the difference of a single percentage point of interest on a $17,000 vehicle can cost you over $800.

Shop around for your best loan. Call local banks and credit unions, and check with car dealers to see if any special factory-subsidized financing programs are in effect.

Make your first visit when the dealership is closed. If you're still at the browsing stage and want to check out a vehicle's available colors and interiors, sticker prices, and so on, you're usually better off inspecting the cars on the dealer's lot at your own pace.

Maintain control over the situation from the moment you enter the showroom. Once you've decided to take the plunge, you'll need to keep your wits about you at all times as you begin the car-buying process. If you've already arranged financing, don't tell the salesperson at this point. The sales manager may hold out for a greater "front end" profit on the price if he or she knows the dealer will be making less on the "back end" of the deal by not arranging financing for you.

Beware the "back end" of the deal. Avoid such add-ons as extended-warranty plans, accident- and health-insurance policies, dealer-service packages, anti-theft window etching, fabric protection, rustproofing, and almost every high-markup item the dealer will try to sell you. Buying these could raise your monthly payment by $50 to $100 or more.

Planning Early to Meet College Expenses

If you think your kids are already sending you to the poorhouse, take a deep breath. Next to buying a home, paying for college will probably be a parent's most daunting expense. Whether your child is a toddler or teen, you should be saving now—with an investment strategy that won't wipe out your retirement kitty.

For students entering the hallowed halls, four years of tuition, room, and board will average around $80,000 at a private college and nearly $40,000 at a public one. Expect an annual increase of 7% into the 21st century. State schools may raise tuition more, pressed by cuts in government support.

What's a conscientious parent to do? Start early, save regularly, and don't feel guilty about putting aside only a portion of your child's education bill. You will make top grades if you save about half of college costs. You don't need to sacrifice your own future retirement pot and lifestyle. Think of college savings as like buying a house, where you just put down a portion in cash and then look for ways to bridge the gap.

How can you save even half of college costs? One spouse may need to work at a second job. You may start a side-business. A job for a non-employed spouse will often be required. Adequate college funds will rarely be accumulated without hard work by both spouses and wise investing. The younger your child, the more aggressive your investment portfolio should be. Since stocks have generally outperformed all other financial investments over time, you should put a hefty percentage of your money in them. If you have young kids, put 50% to 100% of a college portfolio in growth-oriented stocks and mutual funds.

As your child reaches age 14 or so, start shifting your savings out of stocks into more stable investments—intermediate-term bond funds and other fixed-income securities. You might try buying securities with maturity dates that match your tuition payments so you won't be stuck with a bond selling below par just when you need to cash it in.

If 60% of the portfolio is invested in stocks when your child is age 14, transfer 25% annually from the equity portion. *The goal: Be out of stocks and into more predictable investments like money market funds and short-term bonds by the time your child enters college.* You don't want to be in a situation where your child might not be able to enter college because the market crashes a week before tuition is due.

Common College-Funding Mistakes

• **Waiting to start saving.** The sooner you begin saving, the more opportunity the money will have to grow. Have an amount transferred automatically every month from your checking account to an earmarked account.

• **Assuming that you're not eligible for financial aid.** Many people don't even apply because they believe they are not eligible if they earn more than $75,000 a year or own their own homes. There is no real income cut-off. Financial aid is awarded based on a complex formula.

• **Avoiding the stock market.** Equities are the one long-term investment that can defy the ravages of inflation. But the stock market is volatile, so you may want to consider selling part of that portfolio and taking profits as your child enters his mid-teens.

College-Funding Tip • • • • • • • • • • • • • • • •

When it's time to pay for college, don't sell your appreciated stocks or mutual-fund shares. Give them to your kids, who could sell them to pay college bills. Each child will probably owe tax at 15%—big improvement on the 28% capital gains tax you'll likely face. That will reduce your cost of tuition funding. You and your spouse can each give up to $10,000 in gifts per child per year, tax-free.

Be careful when considering many of the most common "college investment" strategies such as variable and universal life insurance policies, zero-coupon bonds, and prepaid tuition plans. Often, the high commissions, the investment risk, or a lack of flexibility in selecting the school of your choice more than offset the tax benefits. Many investment products sold on commission offer nothing special for college savers except for the name. You must look past the hype and focus on the investment merits.

Investing for college is not any different from investing for any other long-term goal. It is an attainable one if a sound plan is put in place early enough. One sound strategy is a dollar-cost-averaging approach to investing in growth mutual funds. This strategy passes three important tests. *First,* you are attempting to fund an expense that will rise with inflation via an investment that historically has outpaced inflation. Fixed-income investments, like savings accounts and U.S. Series EE bonds, fail this test.

Second, dollar-cost-averaging mechanically guides your investing so you acquire more shares when they are more attractively priced. You don't have to worry about timing. And *third,* it allows you to begin with small amounts. This helps you to begin sooner rather than later so you can take greater advantage of the principle of compounding.

You might consider taking advantage of the so-called "kiddie tax" exemption and set up a custodial account. For children under age 14, the first $600 of investment income is tax-free, and the next $600 is taxed at 15%. Anything over $1,200 is taxed at the parents' rate. But once the child reaches age 14, all investment income gets taxed at his presumably lower rate.

The biggest debate among parents is whether to keep savings in the child's name. Putting too much savings directly in your child's name can be dangerous. With custodial accounts, your child legally gains control of the money at age 18 or 21 (depending on the state where you live) and can do whatever he wants—including not go to college.

And if your child might qualify for financial aid, saving in his name could kill his eligibility. You could set up a trust that would require the savings be spent only for education, but the legal expense (around $1,000) and the hassle of filing annual tax returns outweigh most tax benefits unless your estate is large.

Resources for College Planning •••••••••••••••

- **The Federal Student Aid Information Center** (P.O. Box 84, Washington, DC 20044; (800-433-3243) will mail you The Student Guide, a free booklet on the government's major student aid sources, including the Pell Grant Program, the PLUS(Parent Loans to Undergraduate Students) Program, and Federal Work/Study Loans.
- **Paying Less for College 1994** (Peterson's, $23.95) is an indispensable guide for bargain shoppers that reveals how much financially aided freshman at 1,600 schools actually pay and gives answers to financial aid questions. To order, call 800-338-3282.
- **Need a Lift?** This brochure, published annually by the **American Legion,** lists lesser-known scholarships. Send $2.00 to The American Legion, Attn.: Emblem Sales, P.O.Box 1050, Indianapolis, IN 46206.

Even with sterling intentions and investment plans, many parents will still have to borrow when college comes around the bend. Your best bet is probably to take out a tax-deductible home-equity loan. Check how much your employer lets you borrow against your 401(k) plan. Federal PLUS program loans are available regardless of your income.

Slow and Steady Ways to Build Your Cash

Procrastination is pure poison for savers. If you begin now and put away $250 a month in an account earning 3% after taxes, you will have $16,402 in just five years. Wait until this time next

---

Savings-Smart Tip • • • • • • • • • • • • • •

Take 10% of the cash you have left at the end of each day in your pocket or purse and put it in your savings or investment fund. This painless "pickpocketing" could help you save and invest an extra $50 to $100 per month.

---

year to begin saving that amount, and you'll accumulate only $12,733 by the same date.

Those figures alone might give you the incentive to start setting aside a fixed amount each month, but will you stick to it? To protect yourself against yielding to moments of weakness, you can enroll in plans that will automatically deduct a predetermined amount from your salary or checking account each month and put the money in investments of your choice. These plans make saving a relatively painless proposition: You rarely miss cash that you have never actually had a chance to spend.

You may find it hard to save—for a home . . . children's college education . . . retirement—though your parents were able to do it quite easily.

The key to keeping more of what you earn is *self-discipline*—not self-denial. First, get a clear picture of your cash-spending and your cash-earning potential. Then use discipline:

- **Take all credit cards—except one for emergencies—out of your wallet.** Cancel multiple Visas and MasterCards. Don't let them become a way to finance your daily living.
- **Don't carry your checkbook around.** Write yourself one allowance check every week . . . for lunches, newspapers and magazines, groceries, drycleaning and laundering. Cash the check—and don't spend more than that for those expenses during the week. Become your own banker, and learn how to say no.
- **Make a list of your outstanding credit-card debts.** Pay them off one at a time. Celebrate when you finish paying off the outstanding debt by cutting your card in half.
- **Use automatic deductions.** No matter how strapped for cash you feel you are, authorize automatic deductions from your salary for 401(k)

savings or other company retirement programs.

- **Don't carry around too much cash—you tend to spend it.** Automated teller machines (ATMs) have become a convenient source of impulse cash for many people. Try to go to your ATM only as planned, not to pocket an extra $100. If you face an emergency, fine. But don't run to the machine just to buy an unbudgeted coat on sale nearby.

- **Avoid shopping retail.** There's no reason to pay an outrageous markup on retail items when great outlet shops are often less than 30 minutes from your home. You can pick up a local outlet guide at a bookstore.

- **Track where your money goes.** You start out with $40 in your wallet, buy a few things here and a few things there and the next thing you know, it's all gone. Sound familiar?

  Get yourself a spiral notebook. Then write down every penny you spend for two months. When you buy a candy bar from the vending machine at work, write it down. When you write your mortgage check, note it in the book. At the end of each of the two months, review your expenses and label them "O" for optional and "E" for essential. The challenge is to eliminate the optional expenses that give you the least value for your money.

- **Select a long-distance calling program with the maximum savings.** *AT&T* and other long-distance carriers generally will not call you and offer to discount your telephone bill. You have to call them and ask which calling program will save you the most money. You may save up to 25% per month.

- **Cut your homeowners insurance by increasing your deductibles.**

- **Reduce auto expenses.** Buy a used car, or a new

Telephone-Smart Tip
●●●●●●●●●●●●●●●●●●

Send $2 and a self-addressed, stamped envelope to the Telecommunications Research and Action Center (P.O. Box 12038, Washington, D.C. 20005) to receive a comparison of rates for the five biggest carriers.

car you can maintain for 10 years. Getting rid of your car after a couple of years is simply throwing away money. If you trade in your cars every 10 years, you may be able to retire on the same income five years sooner than if you trade in cars every three years.

- **Save money on auto insurance.** Increase collision insurance deductibles to $500 (providing you can afford it) to lower your total auto premium by more than 10%.

  Call your insurance agent to check on rates before you buy a car. Premiums for some cars, especially if driven by your children under 24 years of age, can run up to several hundred dollars a month.

- **Buy big-ticket items out of season.** Air conditioners are like swimsuits. When the temperature goes down, so do prices.

- **Cancel service contracts.** Most service contracts, especially the extended variety, are a waste of money. Don't sign up for them. If you have them now, cancel them including those on autos, computers, electronics, washer and dryer.

Avoiding Common Financial-Planning Mistakes

Here are some of the most common financial-planning mistakes that so many people make over and over again:

- **Panic selling of stocks when the Dow plunges suddenly.** It is typically the unsophisticated investors who sell out when the market takes a big drop. Sudden drops are the time to buy, not sell.

- **Increasing personal debt.** Too many families borrow money liberally, assuming that good times will last forever. It is very common to find families with a second mortgage on their homes, two car loans, and a fistfull of credit card loans. These families are very vulnerable during bad economic times. Break old habits and use personal debts sparingly.

- **Not planning for the big college expenses that are coming.** True, the price tag is overwhelming, but ignoring the problem will not make it go away. The earlier you start socking away some money for your children's college education, the more likely it is that you will be able to swing it.

  One way to get in the habit is to view this expense as if it were a typical mortgage, and to set aside money every month as if you were making a mortgage payment.

- **Not knowing what is enough.** Too many people push for a greater return on their investment even when the push to make more requires over-reaching—taking risks that can result in less rather than more. If retirement income needs can be met with an investment that is safely earning 6%, why take a big risk to earn 20%? When you have enough, you can relax and be satisfied, but you don't have to push for more.

- **Concentrating on finances instead of on personal goals.** Too often, financial planning is based strictly on managing assets instead of on aligning your personal finances with your personal goals. *Life planning must come before financial planning.*

- **Not asking what could go wrong.** Before making any investment, you should know about the downside. What could go wrong? What would be the cause of trouble? What is the probability? How can you prevent or minimize risk? *The best surprise is no surprise.*

- **Giving Uncle Sam a free loan.** You're better off owing taxes than getting a big refund from the IRS. It's a choice between having your money now or giving it to the government week by week just so you can get it back in a lump sum next April. Each dollar withheld from your paycheck is one less dollar you have for investing.

  But don't have too little taken from your wages or Uncle Sam will hit you with a penalty on the difference between what you owe and what was withheld.

- **Getting ambushed.** An unexpected big-ticket expense can shoot your finances out of the water. The only way to cover yourself is to put aside an emergency reserve of three- to six-months' living expenses.

   The key: After paying your tithe and offerings, pay yourself next. Set up a separate account from your regular savings or checking account. Each month write a check to that account. Better yet, look into an automatic plan—have a set amount automatically transferred every payday from your checking account to a savings account or mutual fund account. Other tricks:

   ▪ Getting a raise? Ignore it. Have the difference between your old paycheck and new one put into savings.

   ▪ When you've finally paid off an installment debt, like a car loan, keep writing monthly checks for the same amount—but make them out to your savings account.

   ▪ If you're saving for a new car, keep that separate. Too many people think that they are keeping an emergency cash reserve, when it's really just money for their next car. You need to have both.

- **Being impatient.** The surest way to get poor is to try to get rich quick:

   ▪ Don't move your money in and out of markets and investments trying to anticipate price swings. Frequent trading complicates your taxes and piles up broker's fees.

   ▪ Put your money into an investment over time rather than all at once. That reduces the risk of buying at a high point and losing from there.

   ▪ Buy individual stocks only after you've built a base of interest-bearing investments and a conservative stock mutual fund.

- **Doing nothing.** Some people don't understand money, so they bury their head in the sand and do nothing. In these days of fast-changing economic conditions, doing nothing can be as damaging as doing the wrong thing.

Study Guide Questions

1. How can you and your spouse reconcile differing styles of money management?

2. What are some basic guidelines for paying an allowance to children?

3. What are several ways to teach Christian values to your children concerning money?

4. What financial information should you share with adult children?

5. How can you keep housing expenses from consuming too much of your disposable income?

6. Which is better for you—to buy or lease a car?

7. How can you accumulate a portion or all of the money to fund college expenses for your children?

8. What are some ways you can spend less money?

9. How can you save more of your money?

10. How can you avoid financial planning mistakes that are frequently made?

Developing Your Financial Blueprint

"Suppose one of you wants to build a tower. Will he not first sit down and estimate the cost to see if he has enough money to complete it? For if he lays the foundation and is not able to finish it, everyone who sees it will ridicule him, saying, 'This fellow began to build and was not able to finish.'"
Luke 14:28-30

▶ Where Are You Now?

▶ Everyone Needs a Plan

▶ Living Within Your Means

▶ Setting Your Records Straight

▶ Working Through the Fringe Benefit Puzzle

▶ Software for Easy Money-Management

▶ Plotting Your Course

Personal finances seem to be like a mass of mosaic tile with many pieces missing and little clear understanding of how it all fits together into a coherent picture.

But personal finance is not brain surgery. Personal finance is very simple if you stay with simple things—Treasury bills, certificates of deposit, well-diversified stock-owning mutual funds (U.S. and foreign), municipal bonds if you are in a high tax bracket, and maybe a piece of property. That's it. None of these is complicated. All are things that you can manage personally and manage well.

The secret of personal finance is that *there is no secret*. Whether it's a newsletter, book, or financial column, no one has a magic wand that's going to make you rich.

Contrary to popular opinion, managing your own money is *not* impossible. All you need is time and discipline. What will bring you financial health over the long run is everything your parents told you. Use a balanced approach. *Tithe* and then some. *Put money aside* regularly. *Invest* for the long term. *Trust stocks and stock funds*, because over 5 years or more they should do better than anything else. These are not things you need an expert for.

A man who has one watch knows what time it is. A man who has two watches is never quite sure.

Where Are You Now?

How much are you worth? How much money do you owe? Before you can determine how to improve your financial condition, you must take inventory of where you are right now. You are probably much better off than you think!

To find your *net worth*, add up the total sales value of what you already own, *your assets*, and subtract the amount of debt you owe, *your liabilities*. The bottom line is your net worth. It is a snapshot in time, good only for the moment you calculate it. Your first statement gives you a benchmark to compare yourself against as your

Plan ahead— it wasn't raining when Noah built the ark.

net worth grows over the years.

Even if you do not find yourself pleasantly surprised, at least you have a head start in knowing what it is going to take to plan your financial future.

When to Figure Your Net Worth?

Calculate your net worth at least once a year. Tax time is often good because you have your records out and organized anyway. Be sure to make a separate calculation of your financial assets—the subtotal that excludes your house, car, and other belongings that don't produce income. Use a form similar to the one shown on page 49.

Everyone Needs a Plan

Designate your financial goals on page 51, using (1) to indicate the most important, (2) as second in importance and so on, for each time frame indicated. Certain objectives may be assigned the same level of priority within the same time period. For example, buying a house and having children can each rank #1 in the medium-term column.

As you set your specific financial objectives, avoid these counterproductive money myths:

- **Savings myth.** Simple formulas—like saving 10% of your pretax income—don't work for most people. Saving for some unnamed and unspecified future need is not incentive enough.

  It is better to plan ahead and save for specific purchases—a car, furniture, home improvements, even retirement. One couple that grosses $150,000 a year may not be able to save $50 a month. While another couple who grosses only $60,000 may save 10% by setting aside a specific amount every month for each need.

- **Tax myth.** Although there are still a few tax-saving strategies (home mortgage interest deductions, retirement plans), taxes never warrant making decisions without considering the underlying economics. Getting a tax deduction does

"Money management is not so much a technique as it is an attitude. Unless one achieves self-control, he is no more likely to control his money than he is to discipline his habits or his time. Undisciplined money usually spells an undisciplined person."
Robert J. Hastings

What Are You Worth?

ASSETS (at sales value)

Cash (checking, money-market accounts,
savings, CDs) ....$ _____

Invested Assets .... _____

    Insurance and Annuities............................ _____

    Stocks and Stock Mutual Funds.................. _____

    Bonds and Bond Mutual Funds .... _____

    Partnerships... _____

    Residence .... _____

    Other Real Estate...................................... _____

    Notes and Trust Deeds............................... _____

    IRAs and Other Retirement Accounts........... _____

    Other Assets... _____

        Total Invested Assets $ _____

Personal Assets

    Furnishings ....$ _____

    Automobiles.. _____

    Collections .... _____

    Other... _____

        Total Personal Assets $ _____

TOTAL ASSETS $ _____

LIABILITIES

Secured Liabilities

    Mortgage on Residence ....$ _____

    Automobile Loans .... _____

    Notes and Trust Deeds............................... _____

    Loans Against Life Insurance .... _____

    Other... _____

        Total Secured Liabilities $ _____

Unsecured Liabilities

    Charge Account Balances.............................$ _____

    Bills Due.. _____

    Personal Loans .... _____

    Other... _____

        Total Unsecured Liabilities $ _____

TOTAL LIABILITIES $ _____

    TOTAL ASSETS $ _____

    – TOTAL LIABILITIES $ _____

    = TOTAL NET WORTH $ _____

not mean the deductible expense is free.

- **Investment myth.** We have been conditioned to believe that becoming more responsible about finances means learning about investments. But premature attention to the incredible array of investments distracts us from the real issues of spending and planning, which we must master in order to have money to invest.
- **Myth of enough.** The notion that a certain amount of money will solve all our financial problems, is one of the most anesthetizing of the lies we tell ourselves. Whatever amount of money you dream about, chances are it would not be enough for what you have in mind. More money rarely results in financial security.

Many people seem incapable of keeping a budget. You will probably spend the money you see in your checkbook. So you need a way to get some money out of the account.

People tend to do all right with their regular monthly bills. But then a big item comes along, like a vacation, and they don't have the money to pay for it. So they put it on their credit cards.

Use a three-account system to put your budget on automatic pilot. Here's how:

1. **Keep a checking account at a bank, savings and loan, or credit union.** Your paychecks go into this account, which covers your regular household bills.
2. **Open a money-market mutual fund that lets you write checks on your fund account.** Or, use a bank money-market deposit account. This is for big bills that turn up irregularly—like quarterly life insurance premiums, vacations, Christmas presents, estimated taxes, or household repairs.

Go through your checkbook to see what you're spending annually on these "regular, irregular" items. Then divide the total by the number of paychecks you get each year (if you're paid biweekly, divide by 26). Write a personal check for that amount every time you're paid and

What Are Your Goals?

	Short-Term (Within next year)	Medium-Term (Within 5 years)	Long-Term (next 5-10 years)	Longest Term (Over 10 years)
Pay Off Credit Cards	$_____	$_____	$_____	$_____
Build Up Emergency Reserve	_____	_____	_____	_____
Buy a Car	_____	_____	_____	_____
Buy Adequate Insurance	_____	_____	_____	_____
Increase Charitable Giving	_____	_____	_____	_____
Fund IRA or Keogh Account	_____	_____	_____	_____
Create College Fund for Children	_____	_____	_____	_____
Save Down Payment for Home	_____	_____	_____	_____
Make Home Improvements	_____	_____	_____	_____
Take a Dream Vacation	_____	_____	_____	_____
Start a Business	_____	_____	_____	_____
Change Jobs	_____	_____	_____	_____
Make a Charitable Bequest	_____	_____	_____	_____
Pay Off Mortgage Early	_____	_____	_____	_____
Achieve Adequate Retirement Income	_____	_____	_____	_____
Take Early Retirement	_____	_____	_____	_____
Help Child Finance Home	_____	_____	_____	_____
Other				
_____	_____	_____	_____	_____
_____	_____	_____	_____	_____
_____	_____	_____	_____	_____

How Much Will Your Money Be Worth?

• • • • • • • • • • • • • • • • •

Here's how much your money—savings or investments—will be worth in the future. Example: What will $5,000 be worth 15 years from now, assuming a 6% rate of return and ignoring inflation, using this chart?

Multipliers To Calculate Growth of Your Money

Years	3%	6%	9%	12%
5	1.16	1.33	1.53	1.76
10	1.34	1.79	2.36	3.10
15	1.55	2.40	3.64	5.47
20	1.80	3.20	5.60	9.64
25	2.09	4.29	8.62	17.00

Rate

Investment X Multiplier = Future Worth
$5,000   X   2.40   = $12,000

deposit it in your money-market account. When the big bills come in, then you will have the cash to cover them.

Ideally, you want a money-market mutual fund that lets you open an account with $1,000 or less and processes checks written in small amounts. Banks generally charge a fee if your account falls below the minimum, while most money market mutual funds do not.

3. **Establish an investment account.** For beginners, it might be a bank savings account (the money eventually to be reinvested elsewhere). Or it might be a mutual fund. Every time you get a paycheck, write a fixed check to your investment account as well as to your money market account. Or better yet, have amounts directly transferred from your checking account. These accounts are "sacred." By paying into them first, you're achieving two goals: better cash management and future financial independence.

Everything left in your checking account is yours to spend, without worrying about budgeting. Because people usually manage to live on the money in their checkbook, this system imposes a spending discipline that's not immediately apparent.

Put Price Tags on Your Financial Goals

Once you've identified your financial goals—whether a dream house or a sunny retirement—you need to put price tags on them so you'll know how much to set aside.

No one can predict exactly how much prices will rise, but you can come up with a ballpark figure. If inflation soars or drops to zero, you can adjust your savings plan.

- Research how much your goal would cost today. Look at newspaper ads for homes like the one you eventually want. Figure what you'd need to live on if you retired today.
- Decide when you want to achieve those goals. In some cases, such as paying for your child's college, your deadline is set for you. In other cases, such a buying a larger home, you can adjust your timeline based on your current savings balance and your ability to save.
- Estimate how much your goal will cost at the time you want to reach it. The easiest way is to assume inflation will continue at its current pace and add that rate onto the current cost of your goal.

For the past 50 years, inflation has averaged just under 5%. To be on the safe side, use price inflators of 5% to 7% a year.

You can inflate the price on a simple calculator: Multiply today's price by 1 plus the decimal equivalent of the inflation rate. If you expect the price of a $12,000 car to rise by 6% a year for three years, multiply $12,000 by 1.06 to get the first year's price: $12,720. Multiply $12,720, by 1.06 to get the second year's price of $13,483 and

Pump Up Your Savings

Socking away a little each month is the best way to reach your financial goals. The table shows what $1 deposited monthly would grow to in different time periods.

What $1 Deposited Monthly Would Grow To

Years	Rate 3%	6%	9%	12%
1	$12.36	$12.72	$13.08	$13.44
3	38.20	40.50	42.88	45.35
5	65.62	71.70	78.28	85.38
10	141.69	167.66	198.72	235.86
15	229.88	296.07	384.04	501.04
20	332.12	467.91	669.17	968.38
25	450.64	697.88	1,107.89	1,792.01

the third year's price of $14,292.

If you want to use a shortcut, instead of multiplying each year's price by 1.06 and doing that three times, multiply 1.06 by 1.06 by 1.06, then multiply the current price by that result—in this case, 1.191.

- Figure out how much you'd have to save each week, month or year—and at what rate—to reach your goal (see table on page 53).

For example, suppose you wanted to pay cash for a new car in three years, and the car you want costs $12,000 now. Assuming a 6% annual price increase, the car would cost $14,292 in three years. To have that, you'd need to save $353 each month ($14,292 divided by $40.50) and earn 6% a year on your savings.

Living Within Your Means

Now that you know how much you are worth and what your financial goals are, it's time to do a detailed analysis of where your money is coming from and where it is being spent. Complete a cash-flow worksheet like the one on pages 56 and 57. This is not an exercise in wishful thinking; this is a document that will show you, for better or worse, how you are actually earning and spending your money now.

You may not realize where you are spending your money. But you are sure of one thing—that there is little or no money left at the end of the month for savings and investment.

Take Charge

Set up a financial system that revolves around your goals. Keep track of your changing net worth and review each year's planned spending accordingly. Reassess the situation every year to make sure that specific goals still represent your true objectives.

Here are four easy steps to figure your cash flow:

"Make good habits and they will make you."
Parks Cousins

1. **Calculate your monthly take-home pay.** Divide your annual net income by 12 months. This should be your ceiling for fixed and adjustable expenses.

2. **Figure fixed expenses.** They include tithe to your church, rent or house payments, taxes, car payments, insurance, utilities, and basic telephone service. Don't forget the big expenses that may hit only once or twice a year—like car insurance and holiday gifts.

   Certain expenses—heating and air-conditioning bills—soar during certain months. Don't base your budget on the mild weather months when utility bills are lowest. Add up what you spent all last year, add 3% or 4% for increases due to inflation and set aside a twelfth of that each month.

3. **Figure adjustable expenses.** These expenses, usually smaller than fixed ones, can eat up a budget if not watched carefully. They include: groceries, dining out, clothes, travel, entertainment, furniture, long-distance telephone calls, credit card bills, and medical expenses.

   Put savings at the top of this category rather than leaving it until last. Earmark regular amounts as the cost of building a financial future.

4. **Match income and expenses.** This is when you find out where money is leaking out. You may discover you have more to save and invest than you thought. If your budget is seriously out of whack, you need to take a hard look at how much you're spending on big-ticket items like housing and car payments.

Forget About the Joneses!

• • • • • • • • • • • • • • • •

One of the biggest reasons people get into trouble as they climb the income ladder is that they buy the "package deal." Because they have received a big raise, they think they have to buy a more expensive car or a bigger house. This often leads to becoming overextended.

You never know how much debt those other conspicuous consumers may be living with. It might be far more than is wise—more than you could be comfortable with.

"If you spend more than you make, you are spending your future income."
James E. Stowers

What Are Your Cash Flow Needs?

Income	Monthy Average	Annual
Take-home pay—yourself	$	$
—your spouse	$	$
Bonuses (net)	$	$
Self-employment income	$	$
Net income from rental property	$	$
Interest	$	$
Dividends	$	$
Alimony, child support	$	$
Other	$	$
	$	$
Total	$	$

Fixed expenses		
Tithe and other giving	$	$
Savings	$	$
Rent/house payment	$	$
Home insurance	$	$
Property taxes	$	$
Income and social security taxes not withheld by employer(s)	$	$
Alimony, child support	$	$
Car insurance	$	$
Car payment	$	$
Student loan payment	$	$
Other installment and credit card payments	$	$
Basic phone service	$	$
Utilities	$	$
Other	$	$
	$	$
Total	$	$

What Are Your Cash Flow Needs?

Adjustable expenses	Monthy Average	Annual
Groceries	$	$
Entertainment	$	$
Clothes	$	$
Travel	$	$
Vacations	$	$
Medical, dental bills	$	$
Gasoline	$	$
Furniture	$	$
Long-distance telephone	$	$
Trash	$	$
Cable TV	$	$
Laundry/dry cleaning	$	$
Music and other lessons	$	$
Educational expenses	$	$
Day care and babysitting	$	$
Personal care	$	$
Pocket money	$	$
Life insurance premiums	$	$
Hospitalization insurance	$	$
Disability insurance	$	$
Homeowner's/renter's insurance	$	$
Household help	$	$
Household maintenance and repairs	$	$
Yard maintenance and outside help	$	$
Donations to church, charities above tithe	$	$
Subscriptions	$	$
Personal gifts	$	$
Other	$	$
	$	$
Total	**$**	**$**
Surplus or Deficit (Income Minus Outgo)	$	$

Setting Your Records Straight

The actual process of gaining control over your finances does not have to be painful. It should take you a few minutes, once a week at your desk. Once you are organized, you should be able to put your finger on every piece of paper as proof of what has come in and what has gone out.

Organize your routine financial paperwork:

- **Organize the bills.** Put them in a pile—in the order in which they are due. Pay each bill when it comes due—not before—so your money remains in your hands until the last minute. *But pay credit-card bills when received if you are carrying a balance.* The sooner your payments are received the lower the interest expense because interest is figured on the average daily balance.

- **Pay your bills.** Pay your tithe and other offerings first. Then pay your other bills.

    You may use a financial management package on your computer to pay your bills and summarize your expenses by category automatically. Or you may write out the checks manually. Either way, jot down information and questions on the bill statement as they occur to you. Does your utility bill seem higher than usual? How much money would you save if the deductibles on your home or car insurance were increased?

- **File the detached-bill statement.** Write the check number and date it was paid on the statement and put it into a labeled section of an accordion file. About 15 to 20 categories are all you need. Examples of categories are: contributions, auto, clothing, investments, legal, medical and dental, pleasure, taxes, shelter, outside (for garden, lawn mowing, and trash bags), warranties and guarantees, credit-card statements, and household.

- **Code possible tax deductions.** Use a highlighter to mark every bill or expense that could be a tax deduction, especially if you run a side business or are self-employed. At tax time, that process will help speed up your summaries.

Working Through the Fringe-Benefit Puzzle

Your employer's fringe-benefit program should be an integral part of your overall financial plan. If you are self-employed, it is essential for you to set up fringe-benefit plans to provide for your family's security.

Benefit choices may be almost overwhelming. You may have to decide which of two (or more) medical plans to enroll in, whether to participate in the retirement plan (or plans), and if so, how much to invest and how to allocate the money; and which life, disability, and other insurance coverage options you want.

Health Insurance

If you are an employee, you are probably getting more health benefit options and less benefits. As companies seek to control rising costs of medical plans, they are increasingly making changes in medical packages that reduce the dollar value of the coverage, and at the same time shift the cost to employees. This makes it more important than ever for you to make your decisions carefully, to get the most of what your employer is offering. If you want coverage to provide first-dollar benefits, then you must be willing to pay higher premiums.

Medical Reimbursement Accounts

Your employer may have accounts that let you save pretax dollars to pay for the deductible, or unreimbursed, portion of medical and dental expenses, routine physical exams, and eye care (including glasses and contact lenses).

Benefit-Smart Planning

How would you like to use medical expenses and payments for baby-sitters to lower your tax bill? Or set aside thousands of dollars a year for retirement without being taxed on the money—or any income it generates—for years to come? Sounds too good to be true? It is. But it's perfectly legal.

The tax savings in benefit plans usually exceeds the deductions you could take on your income tax return. Not making the right choices with your benefits is like not cashing a couple of your paychecks.

Benefit programs today are a lot like VCRs. They've been engineered with a lot of value-added features, but most users don't get the benefits because they don't take time to read the manual.

Set the amount conservatively that goes into your medical reimbursement account. It operates on a "use it or lose it" concept. The company keeps anything left in the account at the end of the year.

Flexible Benefit Plans

Flexible benefit plans enable you to have money deducted from your paychecks to pay for medical and dental coverage, life and disability insurance expenses, and child care expenses. Your contributions are exempt from federal income tax, Social Security tax, and state taxes in all but Pennsylvania and New Jersey.

It's up to you to decide how to allocate the money in the plan. *For example*, if you are in your 20s, you may be better off foregoing life insurance and instead choosing disability coverage.

Like medical reimbursement accounts, your employer keeps any balance in your flexible-benefit account at calendar-year end.

Enroll in a 401(k), 403(b), or 457 Plan

You may even be your own retirement fund manager. Unlike traditional pension plans, which are managed by investment professionals and guaranteed a predetermined benefit at retirement, these newer plans require you to make your own decisions about how the money is invested—and your retirement security hinges on the quality of the decisions you make.

Your contributions are automatically deducted

What Are 401(k), 403(b), and 457 Plans?
• • • • • • • • • • • • • • •

Employees can make pre-tax contributions to each of these three plans. Your employer withholds the amount you request from your pay and contributes it directly to the plan. The amount contributed is deducted from your gross pay and the net is shown on your Form W-2. For example, you are employed by a for-profit company, your gross pay is $25,000 a year and you make $1,500 of contributions to a 401(k) plan. Your W-2 will show $23,500 ($25,000 less $1,500) as taxable compensation.

- **401(k) Plan.** Available to employees other than employees of nonprofit organizations or state and local governments.
- **403(b) Plan.** Available only to employees of nonprofit organizations such as churches, schools, and hospitals. These plans are sometimes called tax-sheltered annuities (TSAs).
- **457 Plan.** Available only to employees of state and local governments.

from your pay, before taxes, which lowers your taxable income, and the money grows tax-deferred. Some employers contribute 50 cents or more for every dollar you save. Some plans also have tax-free loan provisions, so you can borrow a portion of the money you've saved in the plan.

As you reduce your income that is subject to Social Security tax, you reduce the taxes contributed to Social Security. Because of the method by which Social Security benefits are calculated, your eventual benefits will probably not be significantly affected.

Software for Easy Money-Management

Lose weight. Get a handle on your finances. These are typical New Year's resolutions. Personal computers can't do much about your weight, but they can help you manage your hard-earned money.

Like dieting, managing personal finances requires choosing a program that works for you. While too much heavy-duty accounting may confuse you, a program that skimps on essentials may leave you wanting more.

In all-around money management programs, Intuit's *Quicken* and Andrew Tobias's *Managing Your Money* dominate the market.

If you are primarily concerned with check writing, expense tracking, and

On-Line Services You Can Use . . . .

CompuServe. Basic services: $8.95 per month.

Extended Services: $4.80 to $9.60 per hour includes Official Airline Guide, ABC Worldwide Hotel Guide.

Telephone: 800-848-8199

Prodigy. Basic services: $14.95 per month (includes 2 hours of free pay-per-use). Includes mobile Travel Guide, National Parks of the U.S. West, Ski Guide, Visa/Passport Information, weather.

Additional hours: $3.60 per hour.

Telephone: 800-776-3449

America Online. Basic services: $9.95 for five hours a month.

Additional hours, $3.50. Includes educational, business, leisure, and entertainment services.

Telephone: 800-827-6364

budgeting, take a look at Parsons Technology *MoneyCounts* or *CheckFree*.

If you want to take stock of your financial position now and project where your saving and investment patterns will take you in the future, you will want to consider financial planning software. While *WealthBuilder* is one of the leading packages, *WealthStarter* is a more basic financial planning package.

With the increased affordability of personal computers and the software programs that are now more user-friendly than ever before, you may want to work toward a short-term goal of putting your financial data on computer. Unless you use the computer several hours a week for other work, it is probably not cost efficient to buy a computer just to track your financial data.

Plotting Your Course

You may have been one of the families that got caught up in the consumption and debt binge of the '80s. Now you are asking yourself what will ensure your financial security in the nail-biting '90s and beyond.

Sobering realizations have shaken long-standing assumptions about spending and savings:

- **Your income may not increase every year.** A few decades ago, earnings increased an average of 3% annually *after* inflation. Now most workers barely keep pace with inflation. You can no longer count on steadily rising incomes to boost your living standard and enable you also to salt money away for the future.

Recordkeeping-Smart Tip
• • • • • • • • • • • • • • • •

Use a safe-deposit box for personal papers such as birth and marriage certificates, a list of your valuable possessions, and a video of each room in your house to provide evidence for an insurance claim in case of fire damage.

Don't keep the only copy of your will in the safe-deposit box. The box may be sealed if you die, limiting access to your surviving family—including your spouse—until your will is legally filed for probate.

- **You may be living on the financial edge.** Most middle-class families now depend on two wage earners to meet living expenses. Divorce, job loss, or the death or disability of a spouse can bring financial ruin.

  With nearly 60% of mothers of young children now in the workforce, families must spend money for child care that in the past could have been saved for education. And college costs are rising faster than the rate of inflation.

- **For many people, a secure retirement is a receding dream.** Employers in the '80s cut back on defined-benefit pension plans funded by the employer, which guarantee each retiree a fixed payout based on his final salary and years of service. Many companies have substituted defined-contribution plans—commonly called 401(k), 403(b), or 457 plans—which allow employees to invest their own pretax dollars in a company-sponsored plan, with no assurance as to how much they will ultimately collect.

- **The heyday of high-yielding, low-risk investments has ended.** Your house may still account for the bulk of your net worth. But you can no longer count on the appreciation of your most cherished asset to cushion your retirement. And after-tax CD and money-market yields in the '90s may not even keep pace with inflation.

  For your money management to be worry-free in the '90s, take these steps:

- **Disaster-proof yourself.**

Stages of Financial Maturity

- **Adolescence**—I deserve it. Why can't I have it now? These people are building up debt that will prove to be a hardship later.
- **Young adulthood**—I'm willing to live within my means, but I still want to enjoy the present. I'll work on the future later. Although these people may make some effort to get out of debt, their financial condition is still fragile.
- **Mature adulthood**—I must take steps today to finance tomorrow's spending. These people realize they can't have the whole candy store. They must make choices and manage their money to achieve the most important goals.
- **Old age**—I have done well for myself but will my children simply squander all I've saved?

There is generally a cost to obtain wise counsel. You usually get what you pay for.

After paying off credit card debt, set aside three to six months of after-tax income as a reserve against job loss or a short-term disability.

Start by taking a hard look at monthly expenditures. *The first place to cut: your credit-card debt.* Not only are you being charged interest that is ruinously high, you must pay it with precious after-tax dollars. Dip into your savings, if necessary, to settle the debts. *Do it now!*

- **Invest in a build-wealth-slowly plan.** You might be tempted to take a flier on that "hot stock" Uncle Fred's been touting. Ignore him. The old recipe for building personal wealth is still best: Start early and allow the magic of compound growth to work for you.

- **Your best long-term investment is staring at you in the mirror.** The foundation of your personal financial security is your ability to keep generating income, both in today's uncertain job market and well into your later life. The jobs that offer security and the prospect of steadily rising salaries will go to those with up-to-date skills.

  Instead of thinking of retirement as a time to kick up your feet and rest, you may consider a change in lifestyle that includes some paid employment. A small investment in that vision today—by enrolling in a community college to boost your computer literacy into fluency, say, or mastering a second language—can allow you to reap big returns when you hit your 60s and 70s.

- **Seek wise counsel.** About 250,000 men and women across the U.S. hold themselves out as financial planners. They include stockbrokers, insurance agents, bankers, lawyers, accountants, teachers, firefighters, police officers, a butcher or two, and even a few journalists.

You must do your homework before hiring a financial adviser. Draw up a list of your income, assets, and expenses. Simply collecting that information will help you feel more comfortable about your finances and save you money when you sit down with a planner.

How do you know whom to trust with your finances? The most useful recommendations are likely to come from friends in financial circumstances similar to yours. Professional designations are an indication that a planner has tried to get some training. They do not prove a thing about honesty or integrity.

> ## Questions for Your Financial Planner
>
> - How long have you been a financial planner? Look for at least three years' experience.
> - How are you compensated? If by fees only, what range of fees may I expect? It should usually be between $1,500 and $6,000. If by commissions, how much could I expect to pay to implement the plan you'll create for me?
> - May I see copies of plans you prepared for three clients? (Names and other identifying particulars should be blacked out, of course.)
> - Who will work on my plan? You or a subordinate?
> - Will you help me implement the plan?
> - Are you a Certified Financial Planner (CFP)?
> - Are you registered with the Securities and Exchange Commission? Are you a Registered Investment Adviser? Have you ever been, or are you now, the subject of a disciplinary action? You can check this out by calling the SEC (202-942-8090).

Once you have some referrals of financial advisers from people you trust, be prepared to pay for topnotch help. Planners are compensated in three basic ways: fees, commissions, or a combination of the two.

- **Fee-only planners.** They charge you either a flat rate or by the hour (often $75 to $200 an hour) to create a plan. They have less incentive than commission-based advisers to see that your financial plan is completed.
- **Commission-charging advisers.** Others charge nothing for advice and receive commissions on the products—insurance policies, mutual funds, annuities, and tax shelters—that they sell you. If you use this type of adviser, simply be aware of the

"In spite of the cost of living, it's still very popular."

tremendous potential for conflict of interest that is created when "advisors" sell products that carry commissions. Fee-only planners do not have to navigate the conflicts of interest that commission-charging advisers do.

You should interview two or three planners before making up your mind, and don't be afraid to ask tough questions (see box on page 65). The International Association for Financial Planning (IAFP) and the National Association of Personal Financial Advisors (NAPFA) have each created an interview form that you can take with you or mail to advisers on your list. (For copies of the questionnaires, call IAFP at 800-945-4237 and NAPFA at 800-366-2732.) If an adviser refuses to answer your questions or complete and sign the form, cross him off your list.

Do you need a financial planner? Spending less than you make and investing the rest is not a very strenuous intellectual exercise, and you could easily master it yourself without paying a professional. But do you have the time? And are you willing to? Baring your financial soul to a stranger disciplines you to take an honest look at your situation. And if you are really worried about what you might see, you don't have any time to waste.

Study Guide Questions

1. Why is it important to determine your net worth?

2. What steps can you take to simplify your budget?

3. How can you determine how much you need to invest to reach your goals?

4. Describe what it means to "live within your means."

5. How can you budget fixed and adjustable expenses?

6. What methods do you use to organize your financial paperwork?

7. Why is it important to maximize your employer's fringe benefits?

8. How can you tell if using financial software is right for you?

9. What are some key steps you can take to plot your financial future?

10. How can you determine if a financial adviser is qualified to help you?

Step 4

"The rich rule over the poor, and the borrower is servant to the lender."
Proverbs 22:7

Getting Credit
Where Credit Is Due

▶ Getting Started in the World of Credit

▶ Checking Your Credit Rating

▶ Avoiding the Credit-Card Trap

▶ Borrowing with Caution!

▶ Climbing Out of Debt

▶ When Bankruptcy Seems the Only Way Out

▶ Handling Mortgage Debt

When it's time to pay the bill at a restaurant or buy gasoline at a service station, what do you reach for? If you're like many people, you take out the plastic money, better known as a charge or credit card. You may have purchased this book with your credit card. You probably don't carry substantial amounts of cash. It's not practical, and it can be dangerous.

You can charge lunch and dinner, clothes, transportation, hotels, and maybe even groceries. Some taxi drivers now accept credit cards. At a hospital emergency room, chances are a credit card will be accepted. Name it and you can charge it.

Advertisers paint the illusion that you deserve the best and can have it on credit. If you begin to believe this, *you set the stage for a lifetime of consumer debt problems.*

Products may bring temporary enjoyment, but they can also become a noose around your neck if you cannot repay the debt. Getting into debt is very easy. *Getting out is the hard part.*

In South Dakota, there is an inscription left by a wearied prospector, "I lost my gun. I lost my horse. I am out of food . . . but I've got all the gold I can carry." Material possessions will never bring security. Jesus warned, "Watch out! Be on your guard against all kinds of greed; a man's life does not consist in the abundance of his possessions" (Luke 12:15). Along with the warning He also offered an interesting question, "What good is it for a man to gain the whole world, yet forfeit his soul?" (Mark 8:36). Security is not found in the temporal but in the spiritual—in our relationship with an eternal God through faith in the Lord Jesus Christ.

The Bible is full of references to financial obligations. Our Lord Jesus often used the idea of credit and payment in His parables (Matthew 18:23-35; Luke 7:41-43; Luke 16:1-13).

Assuming a debt is not in itself unscriptural. For example, you take on financial obligations every time you have the electricity connected to your home or have a telephone service installed.

Living today on tomorrow's assets is not based on

"I am going to live within my income this year even if I have to borrow money to do it."
Mark Twain

Good vs. Bad Debt • • • • • • • • • • • • • • • •

- **Good debt:** Borrowing for a long-term investment:
  - Home
  - Education
  - Investment property
- **Bad debt:** Borrowing for consumption:
  - Vacation
  - Clothes
  - Any credit card debt
  - *Any debt that creates family stress*

scriptural principles— this is presumption. Debt relating to assets acquired or funds invested is not unscriptural.

The danger in borrowing money is that you may become over-committed without realizing it, and become saddled with debt you cannot handle. As Jesus said, a wise person will consider whether he has enough funds to meet the obligation he is assuming (Luke 14:28-30).

Becoming mired in debt can hinder your faith in God. When the money isn't there to pay the bills, you may have a tendency to blame God for not fulfilling his promises. You may be tempted to rob God by not paying your tithe. This is the worst step you can take. Never hold back on God!

Getting Started in the World of Credit

You may be one of the people who pay cash for all purchases and you do not have a credit card or an open account with a store. Credit bureaus have little information about you and that is probably the way you want it. If that fits your money lifestyle, that's fine.

But most people view credit as a desirable and important facet of their lives. And building a solid credit rating takes time and effort.

Keep a healthy respect for debt. Instead of saving for a larger down payment on your home, do you pay the minimum down payment and borrow to your limit? It seems like the American thing to do. But Christians should recognize the subtle trap of taking on too much debt.

If you are stuck in the debt quagmire, you may be unable to provide for even the most basic needs of the ones you love. Excessive debt reduces your financial freedom. In turn, your options and flexibility are often limited. Worst of all, the additional financial pressure can easily throw you into a spiritual tailspin.

But there are still ways you can use credit properly to enjoy life—to make a purchase more convenient or to help in an emergency.

How do you get started? Ironically, you have to incur debt in order to prove you can handle debt. Obtaining a credit card is one of the easiest ways to obtain a credit record.

Credit-Smart Tip
• • • • • • • • • • • • • • • •

Most people have a half dozen or more credit cards in their wallet—one is plenty. It's always smart to get rid of excess plastic.

Although easy to abuse, credit cards are also a convenient payment tool. They allow for easy purchasing by telephone or mail. They offer emergency buying power and can be essential when traveling—especially if you want to rent a car.

You may be in college and want to get your first credit card. Or you may be at retirement age and have paid cash all your life but now you want a credit card. Maybe you just divorced and your husband had all the credit cards in his name. Perhaps you have a history of bad credit.

Before applying for your first credit card, make a firm commitment to pay off any balances when you receive your monthly statement. If you repay properly, your credit rating will be improved.

Your First Card

Unless you have bad credit, you can probably get a major credit card by simply completing an application. You may want to visit the bank where your checking and savings accounts are held. Talk to a loan officer or the branch manager to find out if you are eligible for one of their credit cards.

You Have Bad Credit

There are a few credit-card issuers that specialize in providing cards to those with bad credit. The trade-off is a higher interest rate.

A secured credit card may be your only option if you have a bad credit record. Secured cards look and function just like any other credit card. The only difference is, you establish an interest-bearing account at the same time you open the credit card account. You receive a credit line equal to your deposit.

Checking Your Credit Rating

One woman who was turned down for a home-equity loan was outraged to learn that the reason was a five-dollar outstanding debt at a department store. She left the debt unpaid for seven months, figuring that she would wait until she made another charge at the store and then pay off the total debt. But the store was well within its rights to report her to a credit bureau.

If you are a homeowner who routinely makes your mortgage payment after the due date but before the grace period expires, you may be in for a similar surprise. Paying after the due date is paying late, even if you're not charged a late fee.

You have a legal right to find out what your credit report says about you. If you are using credit or making installment payments, you should review your credit report at least once each year. One study showed that 40% of all credit reports contain erroneous information—some of it

---

What's in a Credit Report
• • • • • • • • • • • • • • • •

- **Personal information.** Previous addresses for 5 to 10 years and names and addresses of your previous and present employers,
- **Data on your credit accounts.** When each account was opened, whether you paid on time, and the balance of the account,
- **Public record information.** Such as tax liens and bankruptcies (which may stay on your file for 10 years), and
- **Inquiries.** A listing of everyone who has seen the credit report for the past two years (many do not need your permission to look at your file).

---

quite serious. Applying for a home loan, for example, is not the time to find out that your credit files have been scrambled with someone whose name is the same as yours and has declared bankruptcy. It can take months to correct such a file with the credit bureau.

Requests for credit reports almost always must be in writing. You will give the credit bureau your full name, current address, addresses for the previous five years, phone number, date of birth, Social Security number, and spouse's name.

Check with two or three agencies because one might be correct while the other may have errors. If you have recently been turned down for credit, your report may be free.

Fixing Errors in Your Credit File. Persistent errors made by creditors in reporting to your credit bureau may be appealed. However, faulty credit files that originate with the credit bureau need to be corrected there. You have a right to ask for corrections in your file.

Credit bureaus usually accept documentation proving that an account isn't yours. When all else fails, you have the right to add a 100-word statement to your file indicating that you dispute the information.

Should you fix the little stuff? Some small mistakes are worth correcting—and some aren't.

- **Closed accounts reported as open.** Too many open accounts could cause you to be rejected for credit because it appears you already have too much credit available. Tell the credit bureau that the account was closed at your request.
- **Missing information.** Not every creditor reports to all three credit bureaus, so some accounts could be missing from your reports. If your credit history is relatively sparse, it makes sense to ask the credit bureaus to add an active account on which you have a good payment record.
- **Biographical information.** Credit bureaus readily admit that income, employment, and other biographical information is often out-of-date.

To Contact Credit Bureaus:

- **TRW Information Services**
  Consumer Relations,
  505 City Parkway, West
  Orange, CA 92668
  Phone: 800-422-4879
  (1 copy free annually)

- **TransUnion Credit Information**, National Consumer Relations Disclosure Center,
  25249 Country Club Blvd.
  North Olmsted, OH 44070
  Phone: 312-258-1717
  (Fee $15 for single/$30 joint)

- **Equifax Credit Information**
  Consumer Relations,
  PO Box 740241
  Atlanta, GA 30374-0241
  Phone: 800-685-1111
  (Fee: $8 for each report)

Avoid credit-card debt. Charging on a credit card is good money management if you pay the balance each month.

You can generally let those mistakes slide, since creditors usually rely on other sources to verify income, employment, and other personal data.

Avoiding the Credit Card Trap

There are 110 million credit card holders in the U.S. The average family has 9.6 credit cards. It all seems so easy. You head over to the mall, pick up a few items you don't really need, plop down the plastic on the counter, and it's all yours. No pain, lots of gain, until the bill arrives, that is.

Credit cards are a form of loan made by a bank, merchant, gasoline company, department store, or credit card company. The cost of this credit is considerably higher than a personal loan at a bank or credit union.

When there is a balance due on your credit card, beware of two words that may appear to be your savior: MINIMUM PAYMENT. You run up the interest tab when you accept a card issuer's offer to make a minimum payment, or even to skip a payment. In the mid '80s, minimum payments were usually 4% or 5% of your balance. Now, at a typical 2.5%, they just barely cover the interest. At that rate, it would take over 11 years and $847 in interest to pay off a $1,100 balance on a card charging 15% interest.

While payments on most loans are designed to eventually pay off the balance, credit-card payments are set up to keep you *paying forever*. By making even small extra principal payments, in addition to your minimum monthly payments,

---

How to Earn 23% on Your Money • • • • • • • • • • • • • • • • •

Use your credit cards to earn 23% on your money. Let's say you put $100 in the bank and earned 23%. In one year you'd earn $23. If you are in the 28% federal tax bracket, that would leave you with an after-tax return of $16.56.

But what if you used that $100 to pay off a credit card charging you 16% interest? Since you are using after-tax dollars, you would save $16.00 in finance charges in the course of the year. That's a return of 16%—almost exactly the after-tax return on your 23% investment.

The Pluses and Minuses of Using Credit

Positive

Access to credit allows you to make major expenditures that you couldn't or didn't handle through your savings—an affordable home, home improvements that increase the value of your home, a car, or education for your children.

Investment funds to help you to invest in income-producing real estate, if the property produces enough income to support itself.

The **security** of being able to borrow on a moment's notice to cover an unexpected family emergency.

Convenience for shopping. It allows for easy mail order and telephone shopping.

Safety is an important feature. If your credit card is lost or stolen, the most you can lose is the first $50 of unauthorized charges. If you lose your wallet or purse, chances are slim that you will recover your stash of cash.

Traveling and credit cards go together. You may have difficulty in trying to guarantee your hotel or motel room for a late arrival without using a credit card. Renting a car without a major credit card can also be challenging!

Protection offered by credit cards is often overlooked. Suppose the water pump on your car gives up. You have it replaced at a car dealership and the next day the new water pump dies. If you paid for the work by cash or check, you are depending on the good integrity of the car dealership to correct the problem. If you paid by credit card, and if the dealership will not stand behind their work, you can refuse to pay this item when your credit card statement arrives.

Recordkeeping is improved by having an accounting of your purchases summarized in a monthly statement.

Negative

Misuse of credit can have a negative impact on your relationship with God and your family.

Overspending is so easy with credit cards and charge accounts—spending money for non-essentials.

Overborrowing is the ultimate downside of easy credit. You can overborrow even on necessities if you don't have the ability to repay the loans or credit card balances.

Credit jail may start out as just a bad credit rating followed by repossessions, foreclosure, personal bankruptcy, and lost employment opportunities. The implications of bad credit can last for many years.

you can deal some powerful blows to your credit-card debt.

Here are secrets that your credit-card company probably hasn't told you!

- **You risk being rejected for auto loans and home mortgages if you already have a wallet full of credit cards.**

    If you have ten credit cards, five with significant outstanding balances, and apply for a loan, many lenders will view you as a poor credit risk. Or if your ten credit cards have modest balances but each has a $5,000 credit limit, you could run up $50,000 in debt. Low-rate credit-card issuers look especially hard at your credit history and your ratio of income-to-debt and potential debt.

- **Keep only one credit card.** With the wide acceptance of major credit cards, you only "need" one card. Decide which card you will keep and cancel the rest.

    Make your one card a transaction card for day-to-day purchases, if you plan to pay the balance in full each month. If you don't keep a holdover balance, it doesn't matter how high the interest rate is. In fact, the higher the rate, the more you'll probably save in annual fees.

    If you can't discipline yourself to pay the balance in full each month, you should use a card with a low interest rate even if the annual fee is higher.

- **Say no when your bank increases your credit limit.** Such increases may leave you feeling flattered, but ultimately they may leave you in worse financial shape.

    Higher credit limits bring increased temptation. Many lenders add up your credit lim-

---

A Credit-Card Checklist
• • • • • • • • • • • • • • • •

1. What is the annual percentage rate (APR) on purchases and how it is calculated?
2. Is the APR fixed or variable?
3. Does the company charge a minimum finance charge no matter how small the unpaid balance?
4. What is the fee charged for each cash advance?
5. What is the APR for cash advances? Is it higher than the interest rate for regular purchases?
6. What are the late payment fees?
7. What is the annual fee?

There is no credit card "grace period"— the time you normally have to pay your credit card balance without incurring interest charges—if you carry a balance.

its rather than actual debts, so your new added borrowing power may cause you to be rejected for an important future loan.

- **Transfer the balances from your high interest cards to lower interest ones.** For example it's well worth the effort to transfer your balance from a 15.9% card to one that charges 10.0%—assuming you can make the higher minimum payment.

  But first, find out what the transfer process involves. Some banks provide free transfer checks, while others impose a cash-advance fee that is in addition to interest (which may be 2 to 3 percent higher for cash than for purchases).
- **Tear up the unsolicited "convenience checks."** You only need them to pay off or pay down a higher-interest credit card.
- **Pay your credit card bill when it arrives.** Each day you delay, you increase the "average daily balance" on which the next month's charges will be computed.
- **Pass when the card issuer encourages you to skip payments.** Remember the "interest clock" is still *ticking.*
- **Negotiate your credit-card terms.** Credit-card issuers are often willing to

Where to Find Low-rate Credit Cards • • • • • • • • • • • • • • • •

Get a credit card with low rates if you have a good credit record. Send $4 to BankCard Holders of America, requesting their latest list of low-rate card issuers and those that charge no fees. Address to BHA, 524 Branch Drive, Salem, VA 24153.

A monthly newsletter, CardTrak, lists the credit cards available at the lowest interest rates ($5 per copy; Box 1700, Frederick, MD 21702 or call 301-695-4660).

negotiate terms if you complain loudly or threaten to cancel your card. If you pay their bills on time and charge frequently, you have the best chance of success in negotiating the interest rate or annual fees.

- **Using your credit card abroad may be costly.** Credit-card companies *say* they use the wholesale currency exchange rate—the best rate available. But they don't always do so.
- **Cancel department store cards.** These are easy to obtain, but they often carry the highest rate of all credit cards.

Best Credit Cards for Different Situations

Choose a credit card based on how you will use it. If you choose a card that's inappropriate for your needs, you'll wind up paying more than you should.

- **If you pay your bill in full each month:** Choose a card that lets you earn a rebate on purchases of products and charges few, if any, fees. Don't worry about the interest rate, because you pay no interest.
- **If you carry a monthly balance:** Look for a card with the lowest interest rate. *Money* magazine publishes the lowest interest cards each month.
- **If you travel frequently on business or charge at least $2,000 a year** (and pay your bill in full each month): Choose a low-fee card that gives you frequent-flier miles for every dollar charged.
- **For parents of college students:** If you don't want to co-sign the card, or if students don't want to ask their parents to co-sign, use a card based on the student's own signature. Be sure the student understands that you will not cover the bills, nor will the card issuer expect you to.

Consider a Debit Card

If you want the convenience of a credit card but without the temptation of spending money you don't have, try a debit card. They are offered by many banks and investment firms.

Debit cards look just like credit cards with VISA

Unmanageable debt ties up your future income to *God*—not just to *men*. This is a sin of presumption.

or MasterCard logos on them. But they *act* like your automated teller machine (ATM) card. The debit card is directly connected to your checking account. When you buy something with your debit card, the amount is taken electronically from your checking account within a few days—just like writing a check.

Borrowing with Caution!

Most people can't buy a car with cash. Most can't put their children through college without a loan. Almost no one can buy a house with cash. You may not find it possible, or even desirable, to be totally *debt-free*.

But credit has to be managed. For example, paying off one or more of your credit cards, mortgages, or car loans gives you the freedom to make choices that you can't possibly make if you're chasing the tail of debt liability.

It is important to avoid unmanageable debt. The only thing more urgent than *less debt* is *more financial security.*

Auto Loans

Next to your mortgage, your biggest debt may be your car loan. And if you generally buy a new car as soon as the old car is paid off, you're on a very expensive treadmill. Getting off is a big step toward living debt-free.

Keep the car a few

Determining a Safety Margin on Installment Debt
. . . .

Monthly take-home pay	$4,000
A comfortable installment debt level ($4,000 x 15%)	$ 600
Current monthly installment payments (including car payments)	500
Safety margin	$ 100

years longer. When the loan on the old car is paid off, put the money into a "new-car account" invested in a mutual fund. And have the car-fund payments shifted automatically from a checking account to a mutual fund.

If you must borrow to buy a car, credit unions usually offer the best deals. Their average rate is often about half a percentage point below the banks' and a *full point* below auto finance companies'. Credit unions are not usually open to the general public. To find one that you may be eligible to join, call the *Credit Union National Association* at 800-358-5710.

Home-Equity Loans

A home-equity loan means putting your house on the line, although you'll pay a lower interest rate than on credit-card debt.

It may be good money management for you to take out a home-equity loan to pay off other consumer debt. Many banks offer these loans at the prime rate, or slightly above. It doesn't take a genius to figure that home-equity line interest rates are better than credit-card rates. Of course, your house is *backing* the loan. If you default, you could lose it. But few homeowners default on home-equity loans. In fact, the default rate on home-equity loans is less than half the credit-card default rate.

Home-equity debt has become some of the easiest credit to get. But while home-equity borrowing can make good sense for some people in certain circumstances, it also can be dangerous. It is the *ultimate credit card.*

Consolidate your debt with a home equity or other type of loan only if you can answer **NO** to both of these questions:

- Once you've paid off

WARNING!
Never pledge your IRA or other retirement accounts as collateral for a loan. The IRS will view this as a taxable distribution in the year of the loan.

Monthly Payments per $1,000 of Loan

• • • • • • • • • • • • • • • • •

Annual Percentage Rate (APR)	12 Month	24 Month	36 Month	48 Month	60 Month
8	86.99	45.23	31.34	24.41	20.28
9	87.45	45.68	31.80	24.89	20.76
10	87.92	46.14	32.27	25.36	21.25
11	88.38	46.61	32.74	25.85	21.74

your credit card balances, will you continue buying on credit even when you can't pay off your balances in full each month?

- Are you looking to consolidate debt only to free up more money for spending? If you're going to go further into debt, don't bother.

Many homeowners "go crazy" when they draw on their home equity line. They finance luxury cars, and take expensive European vacations with no intention of repaying (or not being able to repay).

Another pitfall is that one-third of home-equity borrowing is at a variable interest rate. They could soar from current low levels, potentially doubling or tripling the monthly cost. The value of the home (the security for the loan) could also fall, wiping out the borrower's remaining equity.

Borrowing from Yourself

Borrowing against your own resources can be quick and convenient. You may be able to *borrow from a 401(k), 403(b), or other retirement plan* where you work. If you have a cash-value life insurance policy, it may also have loan provisions. Even an IRA can supply short-term cash.

Since you are borrowing from yourself, there is no credit check. Further, since there is no real risk to the lender, these loans can be "dirt cheap."

Borrow against your savings. Another way to borrow from yourself is to *pledge a savings account or certificate of deposit as collateral for a loan.* The interest rate is pegged to the earnings on your savings. The law requires that the rate must be at least one point above what a CD is paying. A 4% CD, for example, might mean a 5% loan.

Why not just spend your savings? For one thing, you might pay less in interest than the early-withdrawal penalty on a CD. There's also a discipline that comes with the loan; you may be more likely to pay it back than to replenish your savings. A CD-backed loan is also a good way to establish credit. You guarantee the loan with your own money, then prove you can pay it back.

"When borrowing money, 4 out of 5 Americans don't shop around for the best deal. Only 20% of those borrowing $500 or more compared interest rates and terms from several sources." Ohio State University survey

Common Borrowing Mistakes

- **Not shopping for the best rates.** People who drive across town to save three cents a gallon on gas will borrow money from a bank simply because it's nearby.

  Meet with representatives from at least three banks to get an idea of the current market rates. And check a variety of institutions—credit unions, savings and loans, or regular banks. You'll pinpoint a low bidder and, armed with knowledge of the market, you can bargain for an even lower rate.

- **Not negotiating the interest rate.** Ideally, a bank should rank every loan according to its exposure to risk, and assign the borrower an interest rate based on that ranking. That's how good banks *used* to do business!

  Today, most banks rank loans by category (personal, auto, student, and so on), and all borrowers are asked to pay the set interest rate assigned to that category. The bank wants you to pay for any lending mistake it makes.

  Although bankers are used to people's taking what's offered, they will respond to a counteroffer.

- **Not negotiating fees.** Although banks don't want it advertised, each of the fees involved in loan transactions is negotiable. And because the fees for a home mortgage may total $6,000 or more, it's good to bargain. It will help if you have a good credit rating and solid bank-account history.

  Be willing to move your accounts to the potential lending bank in exchange for better terms.

- **Showing up unprepared.** An informed presentation tells a loan officer that you are a good business prospect and better prepares you to negotiate.

  For example, when you apply for a car loan, know what kind of car you're going to buy, how much you want to put down, and exactly how long you need the loan. When you request a small-business loan, bring tax returns, an itemized plan for using the loan and paying it back.

Lack of planning indicates a bad risk.

- **Borrowing from debt-consolidation firms or finance companies.** You generally can't borrow your way out of debt. Money borrowed from these companies could cost as much as 25%— much more than your worst credit card! Even if you obtain lower monthly payments, you'll pay much more interest over the long run. Plus, using a finance company puts a "mark" on your credit report.
- **Using bill-paying services.** They tack 10% onto your bill to cover their own fees.

Climbing Out of Debt

What could start out as a light sprinkling of credit-card slips could turn into a downpour of over-due notices and warnings to pay up . . . OR ELSE.

Anything you don't pay for at the time of service is debt. To keep from drowning in red ink, let a battle plan be your umbrella.

The best way to get out of debt is little by little, and this process requires discipline. It almost always means changing your lifestyle and reordering your priorities. Unfortunately, there is no easier or less painful way out.

The following steps to get out of debt are easy to list, yet hard to do:

1. Set a goal. Both spouses need to set the goal and make a commitment to get out of debt.

2. Get organized. Earmark a place to keep your bills and maintain a calendar to help keep track of when bills are due.

3. Choose whether to earn more or spend less. Many people say there's not enough money. Really, they're not making choices.

Troubleshooting
• • • • • • • • • • • • • • • •

The nonprofit Bankcard Holders of America offers a personalized Debt Zapper Report that helps you save interest costs by figuring which bills to pay first, a brochure on reducing credit card debt, and a list of low-interest credit cards. To order, send $15 to BHA Debt Zapper, 524 Branch Drive, Salem, VA 24153.

They buy prestigious cars. They say they're too busy to eat in, so they eat out. That's baloney—no pun intended.

Sit down with your family and create two lists—one of "monthly income" and the other of "monthly expenses." Compare the two. Decide whether to balance your budget by earning more or spending less (or a combination of the two).

To earn more: Get a second job. But more money is not always the answer. Bad money-management habits will often carry over.

To spend less: Cut back on discretionary spending such as food, entertainment, or clothing; clip coupons; ask for cash discounts, especially on major purchases; review insurance policies to eliminate unnecessary coverage.

Bring the family together every few months to check on your progress.

4. Determine where you are. Make a complete list of your assets and liabilities, including home mortgage and car loans.

5. List your resources. This includes anything that can be used to pay bills—income, talent, and skills.

6. Stop going into debt. Be guided by the "theory of the hole." "When you are in a hole, stop digging." Cut up all but one of your credit cards and pay cash for all purchases.

7. Sell some of your assets. Sell items

The Debt Test
• • • • • • • • • • • • • • •

If you answer yes to two or more of these questions, you may be experiencing credit difficulties and should seek assistance:

1. Do you have to get cash advances on credit cards to pay daily expenses?
2. Is your savings cushion inadequate or nonexistent?
3. Are you using credit for services that you used to pay for with cash?
4. Do you need to work overtime or moonlight to keep up with your bills?
5. When you divide your total debt (excluding your mortgage, college loan, and car loan) by your annual after-tax income, do you get a number greater than 0.20 (20%)?
6. Is an increasing percentage of your income going to pay your debt?
7. Are you only making minimum payments on your charge accounts?
8. Are you near or at the limit of your lines of credit?
9. Are you unsure of the amount you owe?
10. If you lost your job, would you be in immediate financial difficulty?

Establishing a good credit record and managing your credit wisely is the best insurance against bankruptcy.

---

that are losing value and replace them with less expensive items; sell items paid for but not used; reevaluate items that have maintenance costs.

8. Develop a repayment plan. Creditors will generally work with you if you provide a repayment plan. Discuss your plan up front with them. Notify creditors at the first sign that you're having a problem. Call creditors before bills are due (they will be much more likely to work with you).

Creditors who cry the loudest may not be the ones who can hurt you the most. Ask what would happen if you didn't pay the bill. Would you lose your property? Would legal action be taken? Likely candidates to be paid first include: the mortgage or rent; loans backed by some collateral; utilities or telephone. Second priorities: credit card and finance companies. Third priorities: other bills.

9. Invest in your revolving debt first. Take your money out of savings accounts and put it where you'll earn the most—in the "debt side" of your portfolio. *Today's highest yielding, safest, interest-earning investments are your debts.* After taxes and inflation, your savings nest egg earns you very little. But if you invest in your credit-card debt, you can save a tax-free bundle (interest savings, as opposed to earnings, aren't taxed).

While invading your emergency funds may seem risky, if you have ready access to cash—via a credit card or home equity line of credit—you'd be covered in the event of a real crisis.

10. Get counseling help. If you can't resolve matters, help is available through a nationwide network of nonprofit counseling agencies that give advice on money management and negotiate with creditors on the consumers' behalf.

11. Stick to your plan until all your debts are repaid. But be patient. It may take you longer to get out of debt than it took you to get into trouble. You can spend money more quickly than you can earn it.

12. Avoid bankruptcy if at all possible. It will haunt your credit record for ten years. It is not the "fresh start" that some tout.

When Bankruptcy Seems the Only Way Out

More than 1,000,000 Americans declare personal bankruptcy each year. Bankruptcy has become a widely accepted remedy for financial problems. The primary types of personal bankruptcy used today are: Chapter 7 and Chapter 13.

Chapter 7 is commonly called straight bankruptcy or liquidation. Under this Chapter, certain types of property (such as tools of your trade, part of the equity in your home, or a certain amount of cash and clothing) are exempt, or protected. That's the property you're allowed to keep. The rest of your property may be converted to cash, which is then divided up and given to your creditors. Your creditors can no longer try to obtain payment from you, even if all your debts were not paid off.

Chapter 13 bankruptcy is often called the *wage earner's plan*. Under Chapter 13, you work out a repayment plan, subject to court approval, that allows you to pay back most or all of your debts within three years.

Should You Consider Bankruptcy?

If your financial situation is severe, you may not have a choice. Your creditors may attach all available assets and force you into involuntary bankruptcy.

But generally the choice is yours whether to file voluntary bankruptcy or try to work your way out of

"The man who removes a mountain begins by carrying away small stones."
Chinese Proverb

debt. Because it is such a serious step, bankruptcy should not be considered **until all other options have been examined.**

Your friends may say that bankruptcy is an easy way to "start over." But many people who have declared voluntary bankruptcy now consider themselves to be financial "lepers"; they can't get credit, their applications to rent apartments or homes are consistently declined; they find it difficult to travel or write checks because they don't have a major credit card, and so on.

Everyone loses in a bankruptcy filing, whether voluntary or involuntary. Your creditors lose much of the money they are owed. You lose self-respect. A Christian should try to turn an otherwise totally negative situation around by committing to repay each legitimate debt, no matter how long it may take.

How does the Bible address bankruptcy? The Scripture is clear in how we should handle our debts so that bankruptcy is not even an issue: *"When you make a vow to God, do not delay in fulfilling it. He has no pleasure in fools; fulfill your vow. It is better not to vow than to make a vow and not fulfill it" (Ecclesiastes 5:4-5).*

Is bankruptcy an option for the Christian? Perhaps, but only as a last resort. Remember, bankruptcy is not an option as a quick-fix to escape debt you legitimately owe. The average family filing for bankruptcy owes less than $5,000. Obligations at this level simply call for some financial sacrifice, *not bankruptcy.*

Repaying Debts Even After Bankruptcy

When a Christian borrows money, he or she has made a *vow* to repay. Psalm 37:21 says *"The wicked borrow and do not repay, but the righteous give generously."* Although bankruptcy may not be prohibited by Scriptures, it is clear that God expects us to pay all our debts—even if we are legally released from them.

A Christian is obligated to repay according to the original terms of the debt, whether a bankruptcy

"Baby boomers go bankrupt more than any other group. Boomers make up 42% of the adult population but 58% of personal bankruptcies. Most common reason: High credit card debt."
Elizabeth Warren, J.D.

is voluntary or involuntary. *"Do not withhold good from those who deserve it, when it is in your power to act" (Proverbs 3:27).*

Lenders will often modify the original terms of the debt if you ask them. They may "forgive" part of the debt, reduce the interest rate, and extend the time to repay.

Handling Mortgage Debt

The Down Payment

One of the major barriers to buying a house is the down payment. This may be as low as 5% of the house value, but more commonly it approaches 10% to 20%. Thus, a $100,000 house may require an initial investment of as much as $20,000, plus closing costs. Closing costs may be as high as several thousand dollars, including loan origination fees (also known as "points") of typically 1% to 3% of the mortgage amount.

Figure Out the "Amount" of House You Can Afford

The amount of down payment and closing costs you will have to accumulate depends upon how much house you can afford. The first thing to do is to get an idea of how large a mortgage you can carry. The following rules of thumb are often used by lenders:

- Your monthly mortgage payment should not exceed more than 28% of your gross pay.
- Your total monthly debt obligations, including the mortgage, should not exceed 36% of your gross monthly income.

There are a variety of loan-affordability measures commonly used by lenders to help you get monthly mortgage payment you can afford.

Estimating Your Mortgage Payments

Use the table on page 89 to estimate the amount of your monthly mortgage payment. For example, if you're considering a $100,000 thirty-year mortgage at 7.5%, multiply 100 times the applicable amount—$7.00 per $1,000 borrowed—to find that your monthly principal and interest payment will be approximately $700.

The reality of how much or how little house they can afford knocks many first-time buyers for a loop. You may have to pull back from the search and rent for another year or two in order to save up enough for your first house.

Coming to Terms with Points

With most lenders, you can get a lower rate by paying an up-front fee of one or two discount points—a percentage of the loan amount. Each point is equal in cost to about one-eighth of one percent interest on a thirty-year mortgage. For example, an 8.5% loan with two points is roughly equivalent to an 8.75% loan with no points.

How do you decide which is best for you? Decide how long you plan to stay in your home. Let's say you can get a $100,000 fixed-rate 30-year mortgage at the terms described above. The monthly payment on the no-point loan would be $787; on the two-point loan, it would be $769. Saving $18 a month, it would take you 111 months to recoup the $2,000 in points. So paying points to get the lower rate would make sense if you planned to stay in the home for at least 111 months.

Adjustable Versus Fixed Rate

The two main types of mortgages are fixed-rate and adjustable-rate mortgages (ARMs). A fixed-rate mortgage is a loan whose rate of interest does not change during the life of the mortgage. As a result,

Monthly Payment per $1,000 of Loan

• • • • • • • • • • • • • • • • • •

	Length of Loan	
Interest Rate	15 Years	30 Years
7.00%	$8.99	$6.66
7.25	9.13	6.83
7.50	9.28	7.00
7.75	9.42	7.17
8.00	9.56	7.34
8.25	9.71	7.52
8.50	9.85	7.69
8.75	10.00	7.87
9.00	10.15	8.05
9.25	10.30	8.23

Fixed Versus Variable Mortgages ● ● ● ● ● ● ● ● ● ● ● ● ● ● ● ● ●

Consider a fixed-rate mortgage when:
- you want predictable housing costs.
- your income is stable.
- you can afford to pay the higher interest rate of a fixed rate mortgage.
- you don't plan to move for at least five years.

Look at an adjustable-rate mortgage when:
- you don't qualify for a fixed rate.
- your income is consistently going up to outrun payment increases.
- the mortgage has low caps on how often and how much the rate can be adjusted.
- you are not planning to stay in the house for more than five years.

your loan payment will be a constant amount. By contrast, an adjustable-rate mortgage is a loan whose interest rate fluctuates throughout the life of the loan.

The main factor in your decision should be how long you plan to stay put: If it's less than five years, the ARM will almost certainly be a better deal. The rate on most ARMs cannot increase more than two percentage points a year and six points over the life of the loan. So even if your rate jumped by the maximum each year, a 4% ARM would cost you less than a 7.3% fixed-rate mortgage over periods of four years or less.

Fifteen-year Versus 30-year Mortgages

The interest rates on 15-year mortgages are usually a quarter to a half percentage point lower than those on comparable 30-year loans. The shorter term slightly reduces the lender's risk. And because you pay off your loan more quickly, you save even more interest costs. The downside: higher monthly payments on the shorter loan. You should not always go for the interest savings if you can afford the higher payments. If you invest the monthly cash freed up by a 30-year loan, your investment earnings may more than offset the extra interest costs.

Invest the 30 versus 15-year mortgage savings in a tax-deferred vehicle like a 401(k), 403(b), 457 plan or an IRA to maximize your earnings power. If you want maximum flexibility for a down payment on your next house or add to a college savings fund, invest it in an account that does not have the withdrawal restrictions of a tax-deferred arrangement.

Want to turn your 30-year mortgage into a 15-

year mortgage at no cost? It's easy. Just make additional principal payments each month on your 30-year mortgage so that it is paid off over the shorter period of time.

Getting the Mortgage You Want

You have a much better chance of arranging for a favorable mortgage if you have maintained a good working relationship with a bank and have a clean credit history. You should get to know a personal banker and keep that person informed of your financial status. Even if you are not currently interested in purchasing a specific house, you should test for your mortgage-borrowing capacity. The banker should be able to gauge whether you are capable of assuming a substantial mortgage and may even be able to bend a few rules if you are a good customer.

If possible, the mortgage you arrange should be assumable—meaning the next owner can assume the existing mortgage at the time of sale. Your agreement should not include a mortgage prepayment penalty, so that you will be able to repay the mortgage early, either with a lump sum or with periodic additional payments. Creditworthy borrowers should not hesitate to try to negotiate concessions on the loan terms.

Mortgage Shopping

In addition to scrutinizing lenders' fees for services rendered, you should compare lenders' mortgage rates. There are usually surprising differences among them. Most local papers list the lenders' rates in their financial sections.

Ask your real estate agent to run a computerized shopping service that can take your search for a suitable mortgage well beyond

Get Comparative Mortgage Rates

You don't have to take a mortgage from a bank in your area. You may be able to get a better deal from an out-of-town lender. For $20, *HSH Associates* (1200 Route 23, Butler, NJ 07405 (800-UPDATES) will send you information on mortgage data from different parts of the country.

your local area. Do some checking on your own. Some agents work exclusively with one or two lenders, who may or may not have the best rates.

Refinancing Your Mortgage

The old advice that refinancing isn't worth it unless you can reduce your rate by two percentage points is too simplistic. Improving your interest rate by as little as a quarter of a point can save you money in the long run—although perhaps not enough to justify the effort. The crucial question is how long you'll be living in your home. If you are planning to remain well beyond the time it would take to recoup your closing costs through lower monthly loan payments, it probably makes sense to refinance.

In addition to closing costs and points, there may be prepayment penalties of up to six months' interest. You can estimate the amount of closing costs by requesting an estimate of closing costs from your lender. You should generally aim to recoup refinancing costs in five years or less.

When Should You Refinance? ●●●●●●●●●●●●●●●●●

Use the following mortgage-refinancing worksheet to determine the number of months it will take for you to break even, should you decide to refinance:

	Example	Your Calculation
1. Present mortgage payment	$1,000	_____
2. Mortgage payment after refinancing	800	_____
3. Monthly savings (subtract line 2 from line 1)	200	_____
4. Total fees, closing costs, and prepayment penalties	2,000	_____
5. Months needed to break even (divide item 4 by item 3)	10	_____

Reverse Mortgages

Your most valuable asset may be the equity in your home. A reverse mortgage allows you to turn your equity into current income. You still have the security of the continued ownership of your home. Instead of borrowing against your equity and paying interest, you contract with a bank to convert some of your home equity to cash while you retain ownership. These are called reverse mortgages because they are the opposite of traditional mortgages—the bank makes payments to you.

With a reverse mortgage you can take your proceeds whenever you want, in a lump sum, in monthly checks, over a fixed time period or as long as you occupy the home. The amount you can borrow depends on your age, the value of the equity in your home, and the interest rate charged by the lender.

> ## *Prepaying Your Mortgage*
> ● ● ● ● ● ● ● ● ● ● ● ● ● ● ● ● ●
>
> **Before you prepay your fixed-rate mortgage:**
> 1. Pay off other debts. They're usually more expensive than mortgages and probably aren't tax deductible.
> 2. Create and fund a retirement plan.
> 3. Create and fund a college investment fund.
> 4. Build up some liquid reserves (but don't go overboard).
> 5. Buy disability-income insurance.

The amount of interest you owe increases every month. Over time, the interest owed can become considerable and your equity stake can shrink dramatically. However, a reverse mortgage can be a good way to use the equity in your home—if you do not mind leaving your heirs a far smaller estate when you die.

All payments you receive from a reverse mortgage are considered nontaxable income. Therefore, they do not lower your Social Security or Medicare benefits. The interest you pay on a reverse mortgage is not tax deductible until you pay off all or part of your total reverse mortgage debt. Repayment generally occurs when you sell the home or at death.

Prepaying Your Mortgage

Conventional wisdom says prepaying your mortgage is smart. Owning a home free and clear is a true status symbol for the 1990s.

Some people should prepay: mainly those who have already funded most of their other financial goals. And anyone who is risk-averse may appreciate the emotional reward of paying off a mortgage— no small consideration in uncertain economic times.

The basic rule of thumb is that you need to find an investment producing a pretax return greater than the mortgage-interest rate (to beat the benefit of paying down the mortgage).

Paying down the mortgage doesn't require a grand gesture like writing one big check to the bank or going on a bread-and-water diet. Instead, it's generally possible to make additional principal payments—each month or whenever the homeowner has the extra money—that will speed the day when the mortgage is paid off.

Each month you have to decide the best place to put your extra money. It is just as easy to prepay a mortgage by $300 as to put $300 in a bond or stock mutual fund. If you can save 10% interest or earn 8% on your investments, you are better off to save 10% interest.

The critical question is, "Can I make more money investing than I am paying on my mortgage?" Although paying off the mortgage probably won't top the returns possible from long-term stock market investments, the numbers can be compelling for investors considering fixed-income investments. Though investing always has some risk, the pay-down of a mortgage has zero risk.

Assuming that mortgage rate and tax consequences are in your favor, there are other factors you must consider when deciding to prepay a mortgage. For example, prepayment also makes sense when:

- **You have discretionary cash.** Don't put money into a mortgage if you need all your income to meet everyday needs.
- **You have enough liquidity.** If you're nearing retirement, you'll also have liquidity concerns. You'll need money to live on after the paychecks stop. Don't make yourself *house-rich* if you'll be *cash-poor*.
- **Your other debts are paid off.** Your low-cost, deductible mortgage debt should be the last debt you prepay. Instead of prepaying your mortgage, prepay all credit-card debt, auto loans, and personal bank loans first. If your Visa or MasterCard provider charges 17%, prepaying that debt is like earning 17%—*risk-free*. Even better, it's like earning 17%, after tax, because the interest on personal debt isn't deductible.

Study Guide Questions

1. What does the Bible teach about assuming and paying obligations?

2. In what ways is a good credit rating important?

3. How can you correct a bad credit rating or report?

4. What are some positive and negative aspects of using credit?

5. If you use credit cards, what are some good "rules" for their use?

6. What is your way of viewing mortgage debt?

7. What are some common borrowing mistakes?

8. What are some steps out of a serious financial problem?

9. Why do you believe bankruptcy is or is not an option for the Christian?

10. How can you determine how much house you can afford?

Step 5

Making Your Life — Less Taxing

▶ Putting the Tax System on Your Side

▶ Planning Ahead to Minimize Taxes

▶ Strategies to Save Taxes

▶ Tax Mistakes to Avoid

▶ Easing the Chore of Preparing Your Returns

▶ Working with the IRS

▶ Taxes and Your Current Giving

Taxes can be a very unpleasant aspect of personal finance. If you concentrate on learning thousands of pages of complex tax laws and regulations, you will surely be overwhelmed. Most obscure tax laws do not apply to you. However, you need a basic understanding of tax strategies, the principles of how your tax return fits together, and basic methods to cut your tax bill. Even if you pay a professional to complete your return, you are the one who must act in a tax-smart manner throughout the year.

It is possible to go overboard on tax-saving strategies. Some of them just aren't worth the effort. A good example is putting money in your child's name to save taxes. The benefits are generally small, and the headaches can be major.

Tax planning is an important part of personal financial planning—but it is just one part. Investment or financial decisions should never be made solely or even primarily on the basis of tax savings.

Run from grandiose tax-savings schemes. These often lack economic substance (in spite of what the colorful brochures tell you). The old adage still holds: *If it sounds too good to be true, it probably is.*

There are a few legitimate tax shelters available like rehabilitation investment credits, low-income housing credits, and oil-well deductions. But even these are almost certainly best left alone. Stick to the basics. Familiarize yourself with the tax-saving advantages of a certain transaction—but don't make your decision solely on the basis of taxes saved.

> *"When there is an income tax, the just man will pay more and the unjust less on the same amount of income."*
> **Plato**

Tax Credo for Christians
• • • • • • • • • • • • • • •

Christians want to pay taxes that are due—no more and no less. The "Render unto Caesar" admonition must be taken seriously. (Actually, the tithe of the Old Testament included some of what we now pay in taxes, especially the "poor tithe.") Practicing tax avoidance—legally reducing taxes to the lowest possible amount—is expected. But tax evasion—the illegal nonpayment of taxes owed—is not a biblical option.

Putting the Tax System on Your Side

"The hardest thing in the world to understand is the income tax."
Albert Einstein

Unless you make at least $140,000 a year as a couple, you are probably in the 15%, 28%, or 31% marginal tax bracket. If you have taxable income of $38,000 or less in 1994, you are in the 15% marginal bracket if filing jointly. The 28% bracket takes you up to $91,850 of taxable income.

A 36% levy kicks in at $140,000 of taxable income for couples—that's minus about $40,000 in deductions and exemptions that folks at these levels can usually subtract. To reach the top stated marginal rate of 39.6% at $250,000 in taxable income, you would probably have to earn over $300,000 a year. The real top rate is as high as 44% when you take into account the loss of deductions and personal exemptions that high-income taxpayers face. This is before considering state income taxes and social security taxes.

All capital gains are taxed at a maximum rate of 28%. **Added bonus:** Capital gains are not taxed until the asset is sold. And capital gains on assets you hold at your death are not taxed at all.

Your Marginal Income Tax Rate

Why is your "marginal" tax rate important to know? The first dollars of your income are

---

Extensions of Time to File Returns and Pay Taxes
• • • • • • • • • • • • • • • •

- **Initial filing extension.** It's easy to obtain a filing extension. You can obtain an automatic four-month extension to file your return—until August 15—by filing IRS Form 4868. You don't even need a reason to request this extension.

    A filing extension does not extend the time you have to pay your tax. You must estimate the tax you will owe and make a corresponding payment with your extension.
- **Second filing extension.** It's more difficult to obtain more time to file past August 15.
- **Payment extension.** You can request a six-month payment extension by filing IRS Form 1127. You will have to show that timely payment will cause "undue hardship."

    Showing that you don't have the cash to pay the tax is not enough to obtain an extension if you can borrow or sell assets to raise what you need. You must show that you have no way of raising the cash without suffering a serious financial loss or other hardship.

If you don't understand the tax system, you will probably pay too much in taxes.

tax-free. You generally have offsets for the standard or itemized deduction and personal exemption to cover several thousands of dollars of taxable income. The key tax rate for your planning is your top rate—that rate which applies to the last dollar of taxable income (gross taxable income less exemptions and itemized or standard deduction) you have.

You must know your filing status to determine your marginal rate. There are different tax rate schedules for: (1) married filing jointly, (2) married filing separately (3) head of household and (4) single.

How much can you save by shifting ordinary income such as interest on CDs into tax-free municipals? You save based on your marginal tax rate. (Check the table on page 167 to compare tax-exempt and taxable yields based on your marginal tax rate.)

For example, using the table on this page, if you are married filing jointly with taxable income of $38,000 to $91,850, your federal marginal tax rate is 28%. You are effectively paying 28% on your last dollars of income—those dollars in excess of $38,000.

If you don't want to worry about figuring your marginal tax rate, ask your accountant what it is. If she can't tell you this number in a flash, you'd better find someone else to prepare your taxes.

Add your marginal state income tax rate

In 1913, when the standard individual tax form (the 1040) was born, the entire federal income-tax law ran just 16 pages. Now, the tax law is more than 1,500 pages long. In the past eight years, there have been 5,000 changes in the law.

Federal Income Tax Brackets and Rates

Singles Taxable Income	Married Filing Jointly Taxable Income	Federal Tax Rate
Less than $22,750	Less than $38,000	15%
$22,750 to $55,100	$38,000 to $91,850	28%
$55,100 to $115,000	$91,850 to $140,000	31%
$115,000 to $250,000	$140,000 to $250,000	36%
Over $250,000	Over $250,000	39.6%

These brackets are annually adjusted.

to the federal rate to determine your combined marginal rate. Only residents of Alaska, Florida, Nevada, South Dakota, Texas, Washington, and Wyoming have no state income taxes at all.

Tax on Social Security Benefits

Retirees must stay alert for the potential tax bite on Social Security benefits. Married retirees who earn more than $44,000 a year ($34,000 for single filers) have to pay income taxes on 85% of their Social Security benefits. Tax-exempt interest is includable in income when calculating the amount of your Social Security benefits that will be taxed.

Planning Ahead to Minimize Taxes

The two basic tax-savings techniques are: delaying payment of taxes, using tax-deferral strategies, and sidestepping taxes altogether. Here are the most popular and practical ways to cut your taxes.

Charitable Contributions

You can accumulate deductions by donating cash or property to qualified charities. If you donate an asset such as stocks, bonds, or real estate that has appreciated sharply, you avoid the capital gains taxes you would have paid, had you sold the asset for a profit, and you qualify for a charitable-contribution deduction on the fair market value of the gift.

Contribution Alert
• • • • • • • • • • • • •

If you give $250 or more in one gift to a charity, you must obtain a receipt for the contribution by the date you file your tax return. You cannot rely on your canceled check as the sole proof of a contribution.

Employee Benefits

You can shelter investment capital from taxes until you retire—when you probably will be in a lower tax bracket—by contributing to Keogh plans,

401(k), 403(b), or 457 salary reduction plans, simplified employee pension (SEP) plans, IRA and profit-sharing plans. Certain fringe benefits, such as the first $50,000 of group life insurance coverage and medical insurance premiums paid by your employer, are not taxed. Many companies also offer flexible spending accounts, which allow you to put aside pretax money to cover certain health care and dependent care costs. All of these employee benefit plans are described in more detail in Step 3.

Growth Stocks and Funds

Because you can determine when you sell a stock or mutual fund and pay tax on the gain, the growth in the value of the asset is, in effect, a *tax shelter*. Particularly if the stock or fund pays little or no dividend, all of the company's profits are reinvested in the business and, hopefully, making the value of the stock or mutual fund rise over time.

Income Shifting

By transferring a tax burden from someone in a high tax bracket to someone in a lower tax bracket, like your child, you can reduce the total amount of taxes your family pays. Of course, there is no income tax deduction for gifts . . . unless given to charity.

For children under age fourteen, any unearned income (investment income such as interest and dividends) the child receives that exceeds $1,200 is taxed at the parents' rate (known as the kiddie tax). When the child turns fourteen, all of his or her unearned income is taxed at the child's rate, but the child can do whatever he or she likes with the money once the child reaches the age of majority, normally eighteen or twenty-one. Most of the benefits of shifting money to family members relates to estate tax savings (see Step 9).

You may make gifts of up to $10,000 each year per individual without any tax consequences; or, if you are married, you and your spouse could each give $10,000 per year to an individual. Gifts of over $10,000 per year may still be wise although there may be some gift or estate tax impact.

If giving securities late in the year, you should endorse them over to the donee. Getting certificates retitled can prove burdensome during the last few days of the calendar year.

If you are giving by check, be sure the recipient deposits the check before year-end, or give them a certified check. Otherwise, it will count as a gift in the subsequent year for gift tax purposes. The income tax rule for checks mailed to a charity is different—the deduction is counted in the year sent.

Insurance

The tax-deferred buildup of cash value in an insurance policy provides a major long-term tax benefit. This applies to whole life, variable life, and universal life policies, as well as to variable and fixed annuities. Unlike IRAs, Keoghs, 401(k), 403(b), or 457 plans, there are no limits on how much you can invest in insurance policies to take advantage of this tax shelter. Life insurance also offers certain tax breaks when benefits are paid out. See Step 6 for more details.

Municipal Bonds

The interest on tax-free municipal bonds is not taxed by the federal government and usually is not taxed by the state government for its residents if the bonds are issued in the state. This often provides a higher after-tax equivalent yield than you can get from a taxable bond of similar quality and maturity. For example, an investor in the 28% federal tax bracket would have to earn over 8.3% on a taxable bond to match a 6% tax-exempt yield.

Municipal-bond

Tax-Planning Tips
• • • • • • • • • • • • • • •

Tax planning differs for each person. However, three rules do apply for all:
- Realize as much of your income as possible when your tax rate is low.
- Conversely, pay deductible expenses in a year when your tax rate is high.
- Taxes paid today cost you more than taxes paid next year, if tax rates remain constant. However, income and social tax rates are probably as low as they will be for years.

interest goes untaxed if it is received through individual bonds, bond mutual funds, or unit investment trusts. See Step 7 for more details.

Real Estate

You can qualify for mortgage interest deductions for the acquisition debt secured by a principal residence, or a second home up to $1 million. In addition, you can deduct the interest you pay on a home-equity credit line up to $100,000, no matter how you spend the proceeds of the loan. You may also deduct property taxes you pay to your locality.

When you sell your home, you can defer capital gains if you reinvest the proceeds in a new home of equal or greater value. If you are age 55 or older, you may be able to exclude (one-time only) the capital gains taxes on up to $125,000 of your profit.

If you rent real estate for a living, you may also merit certain tax benefits. When you actively manage a property you own by finding tenants, collecting rents, and supervising maintenance, you can deduct up to $25,000 in depreciation and other losses, generated by the property. This can help reduce your taxable income.

> ## Defer Tax on Your Home Sale
> • • • • • • • • • • • • • • • •
>
> | | |
> |---|---|
> | Cost of home No. 1 in 1985 | $130,000 |
> | Cost of room added in 1988 | 20,000 |
> | | 150,000 |
> | Net sales price—November 1994 | 175,000 |
> | Gain | $25,000 |
>
> Home No. 2 was purchased in March 1995 for $190,000. The $25,000 gain is deferred.
> If home No. 2 had cost only $160,000, tax would be due on $15,000 ($175,000—$160,000).

You may obtain some tax benefits by buying publicly offered real-estate limited partnerships. However, the days of high-write-off partnerships are long gone. These should generally be avoided.

Starting a Business

As long as you can show the IRS that you are trying to profit from a business venture, many expenses legitimately incurred by your company

Operating your own business is one of the few valid tax shelters available today.

qualify for business-related deductions. For example, you can deduct the business-related portion of your car expenses. *However, if you don't make a profit in three out of five consecutive years, the IRS may claim that you are pursuing a hobby and not running a legitimate business.*

Treasury Bonds

Interest on bonds, bills, and notes issued by the U.S. government, including U.S. savings bonds, is not taxable at the state or local level. This gives these bonds a slightly higher effective yield than other taxable bonds, such as corporate bonds, particularly in states with higher income tax rates.

Trusts

By establishing various kinds of trusts, you can sidestep estate-tax bills. See Step 9, "Passing the Baton," for a more detailed explanation.

Capital-Gains Taxes

If you are building up a solid investment portfolio—and you should be—dealing with the capital gains (a capital gain results from the profitable disposal of most property) tax effectively will be one of your best tax-savings strategies. Some high-income taxpayers are in the 39.6% federal tax bracket starting in 1993. However, the maximum capital-gains rate is only 28%. (There is also income tax on capital gains in most states.)

When an investment rises in value, taxes must be paid only when that property is sold. As long as you hold on to your investments, you don't pay any capital-gains taxes on the increase in value these investments have enjoyed.

Your portfolio may consist largely of either real estate or common stock that has been owned for a long time. These assets may have significant unrealized capital gains (gains that will not be taxed until the assets are sold). The annual rent or dividend income the assets produce can easily be as much as 20% to 30% of their original cost basis. The key to this approach to wealth creation is avoidance of the capital-gains tax by "buying and holding."

Strategies to Save Taxes

Here are several basic tax-planning strategies you can use:

1. Keep meticulous tax records. Unless you want to pay more taxes than you have to, improve your tax record-keeping system. Have a notebook handy to keep track of miscellaneous tax-deductible expenses.

2. If you're owed a refund, send in your tax return early. After all, the federal government isn't going to pay you interest on the refund.

3. Gauge withholding to meet your tax liability. Each year, hordes of taxpayers end up paying more than 10% of their federal income tax liability when they file their returns, subjecting themselves to underpayment penalties on the shortfall. Millions of other taxpayers get refunds that average around $1,000 apiece.

Part of the problem is that these people never manage to get their withholding or estimated tax payments right. And small wonder—trying to get your withholding to come out just right is like trying to pick up a raw egg with a fork.

The Paper Trail That Leads to Bigger Deductions

Tedious as it may be, documenting every conceivable deduction is the key to any tax-saving strategy. Dollars you reinvested in mutual funds, miles you drove as a volunteer or on business, points you paid on a mortgage, days you rented out your vacation home—these things and more may qualify for write-offs if you can back them up.

Before signing off on the itemized deductions, examine your paycheck stubs. The stubs may remind you of automatic payroll deductions for dental or medical insurance, or donations to United Way or other charities.

Make the Most of Stock Losses •••••••••••••••

You may have chalked up capital losses this year on stock investments in an industry you expect to recover at a later date. You can take advantage of the expected recovery by selling the stock of the company in the particular industry to realize a loss this year. Then replace it with a stock that has similar characteristics in the same industry. Just don't sell a stock at a loss and buy the same stock again within 30 days before or after the sale, or you won't be able to realize a loss on stock until you sell it again.

Use last year's tax return as a benchmark. Project changes in your income and deductions. Then file a new Form W-4 with your employer or pay the tax through quarterly estimated tax payments.

4. Take capital losses to offset gains. Capital losses (this occurs when most property is sold at a loss) help to reduce your taxable gains:

- Capital losses are fully deductible against capital gains.
- Net capital losses in excess of gains can be used to offset up to $3,000 of ordinary income annually.
- Excess capital losses can be carried forward indefinitely to be applied against capital gains in future years.

If you are in the 39.6% marginal bracket, be careful about offsetting capital losses against gains. You may be offsetting 28% taxable income with potentially 39.6% taxable losses. It may be better for you to hold onto that loss and take it against ordinary income next year.

5. Minimize taxable gains by selling stock with the highest tax cost (basis). If you've reinvested dividends in a mutual fund (buying new shares at a higher price than your original investment), sell the shares purchased by reinvestment first. These will have a higher basis and your capital gain will be lower than if you had sold the original shares.

You must be able to specifically identify to your broker or fund manager the shares you are selling. If you can't, the IRS requires that you use the first-in, first-out (FIFO) method of identifying the shares you sold.

6. Take deductions for worthless securities.

These are deductible only in the year in which they become worthless. The easiest way to prove that the securities are worthless is to sell the security through your broker for a nominal sum.

If the proceeds from a sale would be less than the cost of the transaction, you don't need an actual sale—a letter from your broker explaining the situation will be enough to satisfy the IRS.

Tax-smart tips

- **Take advantage of flexible spending accounts** to pay for child care and medical expenses in pretax dollars.
- **Use salary reduction plans** like 401(k)s, 403(b)s, or 457s. You can defer a portion of your pay and have the deferrals—and any earnings on them—escape income tax until they are withdrawn.
- **Seek out capital gains.** If you are in the 39.6% marginal rate, the spread between capital gains and ordinary income taxes is a whopping 11.6%.
- **Donate to charity** such assets as stocks, bonds, collectibles, artwork, and other property that has appreciated.
- **Defer tax** when you sell your home for a profit.

---

7. Take advantage of the annual gift-tax exclusion. You can give up to $10,000 each year to an unlimited number of beneficiaries without any gift or estate tax impact. The limit is $20,000 when gifts are made by a married couple. This exclusion is an annual one. You lose it if you don't use it. One reason for making these gifts is to remove the gift amount, and any income on the gift, from your taxable estate. One problem with making gifts to children is that you will lose control over the way the money or property is spent or used.

Commonly Overlooked Deductions

- **Homeowner's Expenses.** Everyone knows that mortgage interest and property taxes are deductible, but did you know that you can also deduct those annoying "points" you pay when you take out a mortgage or refinance? If you refinance, you can't deduct all the points in one year—they must be spread out over the term of the mortgage. Also, remember that if you refinance, any interest prepayment penalties are deductible.
- **Investment expenses.** Expenses you incur to

manage your investment portfolio are tax deductible. This includes investment counsel you pay for in the form of newsletters, magazines, or other publications, and fees paid to management consultants, and investment advisers.

- **Charitable contributions of cash.** You are entitled to deduct cash contributions, provided you can prove the contribution. How do you do this? Keep a current log of your contributions. The log should show the date, the amount contributed, and to whom. Receipts are not required unless a single gift is $250 or more.

- **Fees for prepaying mortgage notes.** Deduct your penalties or fees for prepaying a mortgage or other loan.

- **Mortgage points.** When the points are based upon a percentage of the loan, they are deductible. You can deduct 100% of the points for an original mortgage on your principal residence, but you must amortize points paid on a refinanced mortgage or on any mortgage on your second home over the life of the loan.

Tax Mistakes to Avoid

Everyone has an idea how to save on taxes, whether it's your brother-in-law, some cold-calling broker, or the crew at the water cooler. But that doesn't mean the ideas are any good. Indeed, people do some incredibly stupid things in trying to keep Uncle Sam's hands off their money.

Some people get transfixed on taxes and forget to keep their eye on the bottom line. After all, you can cut your tax 40 cents by not earning that extra dollar, but you'll still be 60 cents poorer.

So, to help keep you from shooting yourself in the foot, here is a look at some of the unwise things done by otherwise bright people in an effort to cut taxes:

1. **Overdoing a tax advantage.** Don't put the wrong investments in IRAs. Topping the list:

Buying tax-free municipal bonds in an individual retirement account.

Many people lose track of the fact that the main advantage of an IRA is that it allows investments to grow tax-deferred until they are withdrawn. Filling them with tax-free investments wastes that advantage.

2. Mutual fund mistakes. Don't buy mutual funds near year-end outside a tax-deferred vehicle, without checking to make sure the fund has already made its year-end distribution of dividends and capital gains. If you purchase shares just before the distribution, your purchase includes an unintended tax liability.

Don't forget about those annual distributions when you sell your shares and end up paying taxes twice. You pay taxes every year on the dividend and capital gains distributions. This adds to your basis in the fund that can be offset against the sales price. Also, don't forget that the cost basis in mutual-fund shares includes the sales fee, or load.

> # Avoid Overpaying Tax on Dividends •••••••••••••••
>
> It is easy to report too much income by not counting reinvested dividends in the cost of sold shares, thus overstating the gain resulting from the sale.

You can report too little income by failing to include gains realized on investment switches made with a fund group during the year. Taxable gains and losses are recognized when stock or bond fund shares are sold and the proceeds are switched into a different fund even if no money is withdrawn from the fund group.

3. Losing a good loss. The year-end process of balancing gains and losses is full of pitfalls. It's so easy to sell a stock just a few days before it would become a long-term (held for 12 months) gain, making it taxable as a short-term gain at ordinary income rates.

4. Too much interest. You may borrow money to make investments thinking that you can write off the interest against your investment income. But often you don't have enough investment income to offset the interest. Investment interest expense can

---

There Are Some Things Even the IRS Doesn't Know ● ● ● ● ● ● ● ● ● ● ● ● ● ● ● ●

If you're a regular wage earner, as opposed to a self-employed taxpayer paying estimated taxes throughout the year, the IRS doesn't know when your tax is being withheld. So if you are running behind on your tax payments for a certain year, you can pay a lump sum in, say, November or December through additional withholding. This could save you a healthy underpayment penalty.

---

only be deducted against dividends and interest.

5. Fear of claiming deductions. Take all your deductions, even if you don't have receipts. Don't leave off deductions because you did not keep the receipts. You may be able to make reasonable estimates of most expenses when you do not have the documentation. A daily diary or appointment book is a good basis for estimates.

6. Paying taxes on nontaxable income. Make sure your dividends are really taxable. Instead of paying dividends out of profits, some companies occasionally dip into capital to pay their shareholders. These payouts are not taxable. Likewise, insurance company "dividends" that return part of the premium you paid aren't taxable.

7. Paying tax on U.S. Savings Bonds used for education expenses. Interest on U.S. Series EE Savings Bonds issued after 1989 is not taxable if the bonds are used to pay the higher education expenses of you, your spouse, or your dependents. There is a phase-out of this exclusion for high-income taxpayers.

8. Intentionally overpaying tax. Don't overpay your tax just because it feels good to get a large refund. You are losing the investment income you could have earned by keeping the overpayment in your own bank or investment account. It is better to make the effort to estimate and pay the correct amount through the year.

9. Not annualizing your income. Estimated taxes are to be paid through four equal quarterly payments. If you have a large gain late in the year and make a correspondingly large estimated payment in the last quarter, you may incur a penalty for not having made estimated payments at an even rate during the year.

Avoid penalties by annualizing estimated payments, an option overlooked by many taxpayers. Under this method, you are required to make estimated payments only as income is earned during the year. Thus, if most income accrues late in the year, estimated payments can be deferred until late in the year. Fill out the annualized installment worksheet on IRS Form 2210 and file it with your return.

10. Taking home-office deductions when you spend only a small amount of time working in that office—even if it's the only office you have.

For expenses to be deductible, the home office must be your principal place of business and the primary focal point for your livelihood.

According to the Supreme Court and the IRS, it means it must be your most important business location. It must be the place where you spend most of your working time and do your most important work.

Easing the Chore of Preparing Your Returns

The mechanics of tax-return preparation can be puzzling and difficult, and nobody is about to give the IRS a special award for its lucid and succinct use of the English language. To make matters worse, the tax rules are always changing.

Many people opt to have their taxes prepared by a professional. If you are a high-income taxpayer, you probably need this kind of help. But thousands of taxpayers should be preparing their own returns. And the best way to learn tax-saving techniques is to prepare your own tax return.

If you own a personal computer or have access to one at work, and have a little skill at operating it, good tax-preparation software could speed and simplify the chore of preparing your taxes. There are many different programs on the market, but any of them are capable of doing the job. The cost of these programs generally ranges from $50 to $100. You

Software That Tackles Tax Chores

TurboTax/MacinTax
- Operating system: DOS, Windows, Macintosh
- Lists at $69.95; $35 in most stores for the federal, $15 to $19.95 for state.
- Number of states covered: 45 in DOS, 20 in Windows and Macintosh

Kiplinger TaxCut
- Operating system: DOS, Windows, Macintosh
- Price: $39.95 for federal, $24.95 for state
- Number of states covered: 23 in DOS and Windows

Andrew Tobias' TaxCut
- Operating system: DOS, Windows, Macintosh
- Price: List $79.95; can be found for $35 to $40 for federal, $29.95 for state
- Number of states covered: 23 in DOS and Windows; 2 in Macintosh

Personal Tax Edge
- Operating system: DOS, Windows
- Price: $19 for federal, $19 for state
- Number of states covered: 42 in DOS and Windows

CA-Simply Tax
- Operating system: DOS, Windows
- Price: Free plus $9.95 shipping and handling for federal $19.95 state
- Number of states covered: 30 in DOS

may also be able to buy a separate program to do your state taxes, although it may not justify the extra expenses if your state taxes are fairly straightforward.

Working with the IRS

Though no one relishes the thought of dealing with the IRS, you may have to someday. The IRS is a lightning rod for criticism—some of it deserved, some overblown. However, if you are organized, come well-prepared, and keep good records, your experience of dealing with the IRS does not have to be totally unpleasant.

When you don't report income that the IRS thinks you received, a computer will send a letter inquiring why you didn't report this revenue. If you don't answer satisfactorily, the IRS will ask you to pay the taxes quickly or face harsh penalties.

Billions in penalties are charged every year and most taxpayers simply pay the bill. If they only knew of their right to demand cancellation of those penalties, many of them could be avoided.

One of the most common penalties is assessed if you underpay your estimated taxes. When you are self-employed or your employer does not withhold enough taxes, you must pay estimated taxes each quarter. How much should you pay? Either 90% of what you will owe, or generally 100% of what you paid the previous year. But what happens when you get to the end of the year and realize you didn't pay enough? The IRS slaps you with a penalty based on current interest rates. You can avoid penalties if your income came in unevenly during the year (use Form 2210), or if underpayment was due to some disaster, casualty, or other unusual circumstance.

Postal Proof
• • • • • • • • • • • • • • •

Using registered or certified U.S. mail is the only way to obtain absolute proof of filing your tax return on time (or at all). Receipts from commercial carriers aren't treated as "prima facie evidence."

An honest tax return is simply giving an accurate account—you include all taxable income and you don't lie about deductions.

If You're Audited

Your chances of being audited are about *one out of one hundred (the rate doubles if you file as self-employed).* If it does happen to you, you will simply need the documents to back up what you claimed on your tax return. Many taxpayers emerge from audits owing no more than they paid originally, and some even receive refunds. The best defense against an audit should be easy for Christians—filing an honest tax return.

The IRS has just three years from the date a return is filed during which to make an assessment of taxes regarding that return. For example, if you filed your 1993 federal income tax return on April 15, 1994, the IRS could no longer audit the return after April 15, 1997.

There is an exception to the statute of limitations if you agree to extend the statute expiration date by voluntarily signing IRS Form 872. Generally you should not sign it. You cannot be forced to sign, and you will not lose your right to appeal if you do not.

Even if you don't hear from the IRS for three years after you submit a return, however, *save a copy of your return and the supporting documents for at least five years.*

If you are selected for an audit, remember your rights:

When You Get an IRS Notice
●●●●●●●●●●●●●●●●●

- **Check your records.** If you failed to report some income, send the form back with your check for tax, interest, and penalties. If you disagree, return the from with a written explanation.
- **Get help from the PRP.** If you have a dispute with the IRS, you may be able to obtain help through the Problem Resolution Program (800-829-1040). PRP personnel have authority to cut through red tape to try to resolve your problem. They can investigate delayed refund checks, unanswered inquiries, or incorrect billing notices.

Relief from IRS Audits

• • • • • • • • • • • • • • •

It's a hassle to get audited once, but some individuals are hit more than once. That's a nuisance, especially when the same items are examined. Fortunately, there is a procedure for taxpayer relief.

A repetitive audit occurs if a taxpayer receives a contact letter from the IRS proposing to audit one or more issues audited in either of the two preceding years. The item(s) to be examined must be the same covered in the earlier audit. If this happens, point it out to the IRS. They are required to suspend the audit and review the files.

- **You do not have to appear at the audit personally.** You have the right to be represented by a tax professional. Most auditors don't even require you to show up; they will complete the audit with your preparer.

- **You have the right to have the audit scheduled at a reasonable time for your convenience.** You can ask the IRS auditor to change the appointment time that may have been set in the initial audit notice.

Many audits do not take place in person but are completed through the mail when you send your documentation to the auditor.

If you personally appear at an audit, bring every piece of documentation the auditor might ask for, such as receipts, bills, and bank records. Answer the auditor's questions respectfully but unemotionally. Don't offer more information than is requested. You may open up a new avenue of inquiry that the auditor had not planned to pursue.

Taxes and Your Current Giving

Your giving is classified in two broad categories: *present* gifts and *deferred* gifts. In present giving, you are making an outright gift. This type of gift requires you to immediately transfer possession and use of the gift property to a charity.

In deferred giving, you also make a current gift. However, the gift is of a *future* interest. Actual possession and use of the gift property by the charity is deferred to some time in future. (Deferred giving is discussed in Step 9, "Passing the Baton.")

Giving Limitations

You cannot deduct an unlimited amount of charitable contributions for income tax purposes in any year. There are limitations based on your adjusted gross income.

The 30% Limitation. Your gifts of appreciated long-term capital-gain property (property owned 12 months or more) are deductible up to 30% of your adjusted gross income.

The 50% Limitation. Your contributions to public charities (other than contributions of long-term capital-gain property) are deductible up to 50% of your adjusted gross income.

Carryover of excess contributions. If your gifts exceed the 30% or 50% limitations, they can be carried over for deduction in the succeeding five years.

Tax-Smart Charitable Giving · · · · · · · · · · · · · · ·

Especially for high-bracket individuals, well-planned charitable giving is one of the few methods left to avoid income taxes. The out-of-pocket cost is $720 if you give $1,000 to the church under the 28% federal tax rate. But if your top tax rate is 39.6%, you get a deduction that now saves $400 in taxes. Therefore, the net after-tax cost is $600.

When Are Contributions Deductible?

A charitable contribution is deductible for income tax purposes when it is actually paid. Payment generally occurs when the gift property is delivered to the charity.

Example ·

A contribution made by *check* is effective when the check is delivered or mailed, as long as it clears the charity's bank in due course.

A contribution made by *bank credit card* is deductible in the year the charge is made. For example, a contribution made by credit card in December is deductible then even if you don't pay off the credit card until January.

A gift of *real estate* is generally effective when

- you deliver a properly executed deed to the charity.
- A gift of *stock* is completed when the stock certificate is properly endorsed and delivered to the charity or the charity's agent.

Donating Appreciated Property

It's often more advantageous to donate appreciated property held long-term (12 months or more) than cash or unappreciated property to a charity. Why? The deduction for appreciated property amounts to current fair market value of property, not the owner's cost basis in property. Be careful never to do this with property in which you have a short-term (property held less than 12 months) gain. If so, you'll be allowed a deduction only for its cost, not its current value.

Under pre-1993 law, certain taxpayers were limited in how much they could deduct when donating appreciated property—property such as stock, real estate, paintings, collectibles, and sculpture whose value increased since being acquired by the donor. This limitation no longer applies.

Appreciated property contributions carry deduction limits. For example, when a taxpayer elects to donate appreciated property that is a long-term capital gain asset to a public charity, the deduction cannot exceed 30% of the taxpayer's adjusted gross income.

Keep in mind, however, that where the value of the contribution exceeds this limitation, excess deductions can be carried over to later tax years.

The IRS also requires a written appraisal of property valued over $5,000 ($10,000 for nonpublicly traded stock), attached to donor's tax return.

Advantage of Donating Appreciated Assets

Let's assume that you have $20,000 in cash and $20,000 worth of AT&T stock and are in the 28% federal income tax bracket. The stock cost you $10,000 and you held it for at least 12 months.

If you sell the stock and donate the $20,000 in cash, you can claim a $20,000 charitable deduction and receive a $5,600 federal income tax benefit. But you incur a capital gain of $10,000 (tax cost of $2,800). By donating the stock, which cost you $10,000, you get the same $5,600 tax savings but avoid the capital-gain tax of $2,800.

Christians do not give just to get a tax deduction. Tax savings related to our giving are merely incidental.

Gifts That Do Not Yield a Current Tax Deduction

It is easy to let our desire to get a charitable deduction for income tax purposes cloud our charitable giving vision. Some individuals may ask for a charitable receipt when paying the tuition of their children at a church-operated school. Or a person may donate their labor and ask for a receipt for the value of their time. Claiming a charitable deducation in either instance is cheating the government.

You are not allowed a current tax deduction (and in some instances, no tax deduction at all) for the following gifts:

1. Conditional gifts. Sometimes a donor will make a gift that is predicated on whether some future event happens—or doesn't happen. Unless the condition is so remote as to be negligible, you are not allowed a current tax deduction.

For example, you give land to charity—but the land will revert back to you after seven years if the charity fails to achieve certain goals. If, at the time of the gift, it is unlikely the charity will be able to meet the goals, you cannot take an immediate tax deduction. When the imposed condition is satisfied or if it is removed, a deduction would then be allowed.

2. Gifts with "strings" attached. No charitable tax deduction is allowed for a gift on which the donor has attached one or more "strings." When you reserve the right to grab a string and pull the gift back in the future, you lose your deduction. To be deductible, a gift must be complete and irrevocable—beyond the future reach of the donor.

For example, you contribute a car to a charity but you reserve the right to get the car back if it is abused. This "string" nixes your charitable tax deduction.

"If you want to have a happy life, take up giving as a hobby when you're young."
Arthur F. Leneham

3. Future interest in property. You may be willing to commit now to make a gift in the future. This is known as a future-interest gift, and it is not currently deductible. It must be a present-interest gift to be deductible.

A future-interest gift becomes deductible when all of the intervening interests expire. That is, when the charity gains full control or ownership of the property.

There is one important exception to this rule. A person may donate a future interest—known as a remainder interest—in a personal residence or farm and get a current tax deduction for the gift. See page 218. (A personal residence does not have to be a principal residence. A vacation home, for example, qualifies.)

4. Use of property. If you permit a charity to use your property rent-free, this does not give you a tax deduction. However, you can deduct any direct out-of-pocket expenses (e.g., utilities) you incur in connection with the charity's use of the property. Expenses that are indirectly connected are not deductible charitable contributions by the owner (e.g., insurance premiums, taxes).

5. Quid pro quo gifts. If you receive goods or services valued at an amount equal to the amount of your donation, no part of the gift is tax-deductible.

For example, for a $50 donation, you receive a book with a retail value of $50. You are not entitled to any charitable deduction. If your donation is $75 and you receive the same book, you may claim $25 as a charitable contribution.

6. Gifts of services. You may not deduct the value of donated services—no matter how valuable those services may be. For example, if you donate services such as electrical or carpentry services or ad space in a newspaper, there is no charitable deduction.

However, you are allowed charitable contribution deductions for out-of-pocket expenses incurred while working for your charity.

Study Guide Questions

1. Explain the difference between tax avoidance and tax evasion.

2. What is your "marginal tax rate" and why is it so important?

3. What is your view of saving taxes today versus deferring taxes until a later year (assuming tax rates will be about the same as they are today)?

4. What are 401(k), 403(b), and 457 tax-deferred accounts and how can you take advantage of them?

5. How can you determine if you would gain from having tax-exempt municipal bond interest?

6. What are capital gains and how does the tax law treat them?

7. Should you purchase tax-free investments for your IRA?

8. What are some "rules" to follow if you are audited?

9. How can you give more by donating appreciated assets?

10. What are some "gifts" that do not yield a current tax deduction or maybe no deduction at all?

Step 6

Your Roadmap Through the Insurance Maze

"If anyone does not provide for his relatives, and especially for his immediate family, he has denied the faith and is worse than an unbeliever."
1 Timothy 5:8

▶ How to Buy Insurance

▶ Buying Insurance to Protect Your Assets

▶ Your Health-Insurance Options

▶ Life-Insurance Solutions for Your Family

▶ The Role of Disability Income Insurance

▶ Who Really Needs a Nursing-Home Policy?

The church bells of the Cathedral of Toul, France, rang continually forty days and nights in mourning the death of King Louis XV. It is said that the resulting vibrations so weakened the bell tower that it swayed—and the bells continued to ring—for over twenty years afterward. Likewise, financial choices you make now will continue to "ring" (even after your death). Wise steward-managers make provisions for the present. They also make decisions that will have a positive impact when their life on earth is over.

Some Christians debate whether buying insurance violates their trust in God. Because of His love for us, God can be trusted to give us wisdom in every situation of life. *But "trusting God" doesn't excuse us from unwise decisions about life's practical concerns—including the purchase of insurance.*

It is possible to "trust in insurance" rather than trusting in God to supply our needs. But a sensible amount of insurance is actually good stewardship of the resources God lends to us.

Insurance is simply joining with others who share a potential loss. If you are the one in that larger group that has a loss, the funds are available to pay for your loss. This reduces the risk that each must bear. *The question you must ask is whether you can bear the potential economic loss alone. If you can, insurance may not be needed.*

God does provide for His own. "In his heart, a man plans his course, but the Lord determines his steps" (Proverbs 16:9). God promises to influence our human wisdom with His heavenly wisdom—as we ask Him in faith. He has given us common sense that we may use in providing for the needs of our family. He has also provided us services that, combined with hard work and wise planning, may be used to protect our losses. Insurance protection is one of the services available to eliminate or limit a potential loss.

There are many types of economic loss and insurance protection against them. Some of those potential losses are quite obvious. For instance, the

"In fair weather prepare for foul."
Thomas Fuller

121

potential of experiencing a major illness or accidental injury, requiring thousands of dollars in medical expenses, has affected many families. Are you presently covered against such loss? Would there be adequate income for your family if one of the breadwinners was suddenly unable to earn an income due to disability or death?

If your home was destroyed by fire, would your insurance cover the loss? If you have a mortgage, you will be required to carry fire and casualty insurance to assure the mortgage holder that your loan would be paid.

You could easily come up with quite a lengthy "worry list" if you gave it much thought. Though you probably won't have enough money to cover all of the "what-ifs" with insurance protection, there is a "short-list" that you may wish to consider.

How Much Insurance Is Enough? How Much Is too Much?

• • • • • • • • • • • • • • • •

To avoid the twin dangers of being overly or inadequately insured:

- Make a list of what you and your family's areas of risk really are and prioritize them.
- Consider what stop gaps you can call on to cover some of these risks aside from insurance.
- Be realistic about how much you can afford to spend for insurance and still be able to save for college expenses, retirement, or other needs.

The first question to ask about potential insurance coverage is this: What potential loss do I need to cover? If the potential loss is small, the coverage may not be needed. For example, if you drive an older automobile, you may not need coverage that will replace it if it is damaged or destroyed (although you will certainly need liability coverage on the auto). If you can afford to replace it out of your current income or savings, save the cost of the insurance premium.

But what if the major income earner in your home dies, or is no longer able to generate income? Your family would probably be left with a substantial loss of income. Without the protection offered by insurance, you may fail in your stewardship responsibilities.

Buying the right kind and amount of insurance is one of a Christian's greatest stewardship challenges. Insurance is probably the least understood and monitored area of personal finance.

How to Buy Insurance

Recent studies have shown that nine in ten Americans purchase and carry the wrong types and amounts of insurance coverage. Policy exclusions and limitations are overwhelming—not to mention the jargon in sales and policy statements. The result is that many people pay more than is necessary for policies or get insurance through companies that are financially weak or with poor reputations for servicing customer's claims.

As a good steward-manager of your insurance dollars, you will be concerned with buying a quality insurance product. You will want to find a company known for good service and one that will offer you a policy at a fair and competitive price. Remember, the least expensive policy is not always the best.

You must do your homework. Learn about the ins and outs of the insurance you are considering. Check the local library for *Best's Insurance Reports* and or other rating publications that rate the financial condition of insurance companies, such as, *Moody's, Duff & Phelps* and *Standard & Poors*. If your compa-

Insurance-Smart Tip

Consider joining the *National Insurance Consumer Organization (NICO)*. NICO is a nonprofit national organization, whose sole purpose is to be an advocate for, and provide assistance to, insurance consumers. Depending on the type of insurance, NICO may also be able to recommend specific companies that are doing a good job. NICO offers their service for a $40 or less tax-deductible donation. For more information, contact: NICO, P.O. Box 15492, Alexandria, Virginia 22309.

ny is rated in the top two rating categories of at least two of the rating publications, you can rest better. Don't take for granted that your company will always have a high rating. Check its rating each year. And if there is a drop in rating, be prepared to ask your agent why their ratings have changed. *Consumer Reports* magazine often makes comparisons of various insurance products.

What Drives Insurance Costs?

Three factors drive insurance costs:

- **Probability that a loss will occur.** The higher the likelihood that an incident will occur, the greater is the risk to the insurance company and the higher the premium.
- **Potential size of the claim.** The higher the potential size of the out-of-pocket loss to the insurance company, the higher the premium.
- **Portion of the loss the insurance company must pay.** If you share the exposure with the insurance company, premiums will be lower than if the company is liable for 100% of a loss.

How to Cut Your Insurance Costs

Get the most insurance for your premium dollars. Unless you have unlimited finances, you will probably need to prioritize your insurance purchases. For example, a broad-based health insurance policy should generally come before a disability policy. In turn, buying disability coverage should come before accidental death travel insurance.

Buy coverage that is comprehensive and catastrophic. Comprehensive coverage will give you a broader umbrella of protection. The catastrophic approach in buying insurance will cover you for the worst-case scenario.

Basic strategies that save your insurance premium dollars are:

1. Take the highest deductible you can afford. Protect yourself from the risk of a major loss. The higher the deductible, the less risk the insurance company is exposed to, and thus the lower your premium will be.

2. Buy broad coverage only. Stay away from narrow policies such as cancer, flight insurance, mortgage and credit-card life, student accident, hospital indemnity, and double-indemnity.

3. Maximize your discounts. They're offered on all kinds of coverage. See page 126.

4. Buy direct. Life insurance is available from an increasing number of companies that sell their policies directly to the public. Just as you can purchase no-load mutual funds directly from an investment company, you also can buy no-load life insurance—with no commission in each instance.

Just as discount stock brokers allow you to buy and sell securities at substantially reduced commissions, California and Florida now permit discount insurance agents (see box on page 140).

5. Buy through a group. Buying health and disability-income insurance through your employer's group plan can be less costly than buying equivalent coverage on your own. The commissions involved in group policies are very low. One caution: While your group health plan may provide some conversion options if you leave your current employer, the group disability policy will probably not follow you to your next job.

Buying Insurance to Protect Your Assets

Auto Insurance

Your automobile insurance isn't really one policy at all. It's a package of six or more different coverages—some required by state law. Those that are optional may not be important to you.

If you have a loan against your car, the lender will want assurance that the loan will be paid if the auto is damaged or destroyed. If an accident is the result of your error, you may have added financial responsibilities. For example, what if someone is injured in the accident? With rampant lawsuits, you need adequate liability protection. The question is not whether you are at fault but whether you will have to pay.

Take advantage of a variety of discounts available on your auto insurance:

- **Multi-car discount**—may apply if all your cars are insured under one policy
- **Multi-policy discount**—may apply if you purchase more than one kind of coverage
- **Good student discount**—for high school or college students with a "B" average or above
- **Driver-education discount**
- **Mature-driver discount**—for those over age 50
- **Good-driver discount**
- **Low-mileage discount**
- **Passive restraints discount**
- **Anti-theft devices**
- **Nonsmoker's and non-drinker's discount**

What Influences Your Auto Insurance Rates?

- **Age.** Since younger drivers tend to be more accident-prone, drivers under the age of 25 pay more in premiums than those aged 25 to 64. At age 65, premiums tend to go up.
- **Gender.** If you are a young, unmarried man, you will generally pay more in premiums than women of the same age.
- **Marital status.** The rates for married drivers are generally lower than for single drivers.
- **Kind of car.** Cars that are expensive to repair and subject to a higher risk of theft will cost more to insure. Check on the premium before you purchase a car.
- **Driving record.** Good drivers generally pay less for insurance.

Shop around for your auto policy. Prices for the same coverage may vary by hundreds of dollars. Get quotes from several insurance agents and from at least one "direct writer," such as *USAA* (800-531-8080). Don't just look for the best prices. Service may vary dramatically.

There are several ways to make sure you are paying the lowest premiums and still getting the coverage you need:

- **Bodily injury liability.** This coverage should be at least $100,000 per person and $300,000 per accident.
- **Buy a low-profile car.** Your rates will be higher if your car is flashy and therefore more

likely to attract thieves.

- **Uninsured motorist and underinsured motorist.** Don't scrimp on these coverages. They generally pay for your injuries in a hit-and-run accident or if the driver at fault has little (or no) insurance. Opt for the same limits as on the bodily injury part.
- **Drop collision or comprehensive coverage on older vehicles.** *Collision* coverage is limited to the value of your car at the time of an accident. *Comprehensive* coverage reimburses you for the value of the car if it is stolen or damaged by a calamity other than an accident (such as fire, hailstorm, vandalism, or colliding with an animal).

  These two types of coverage can account for as much as 45% of your total premium. If your car is worth less than $2,000 to $3,000 or more than 5 years old, you may want to drop the collision and comprehensive coverage. This will greatly reduce your premiums. You would be *self-insuring* your losses.
- **Collision-damage waivers.** These can add 50% to the cost of a car rental, a needless expense when you're probably covered under your own auto-insurance policy. **Caution:** *If you are not carrying comprehensive or collision on your personal auto policy, you have no comprehensive or collision coverage on a rental car.* Your credit card may automatically offer rental-

---

Give Your Auto Policy a Checkup

Here's how a hypothetical motorist could get better catastrophic coverage and decrease premiums. The example, using rates from Economy Fire & Casualty, is for a married 30-year-old husband and wife living in Indianapolis. They drive a 1994 Chevrolet Caprice, and have a clean driving records.

Current Annual Premium	$438
• Boost bodily injury coverage to $100,000 per person/$300,000 per accident from $50,000/$100,000	+ 18
• Boost uninsured-motorist coverage to $100,000/$300,000 from $50,000/$100,000	+ 6
• Raise collision deductible to $250 from $100	- 85
• Raise comprehensive deductible to $250 from $50	- 41
Annual premium for improved policy	$336

127

car protection. Otherwise, you can add a rental-car "rider" to your auto policy at a cost of $25 to $30 per year.

- **Take the highest deductible you can afford.** This is a form of self-insurance. Insurance should be used to protect you from a major loss due to an unforeseen event.

- **Buy a safe car.** Large, four-door models, station wagons, and passenger vans are built to withstand crashes.

- **Buy a good used car.** A good-quality used car not only costs less than a new one, it also costs less to insure.

- **Don't report all claims to your insurer.** If your claim is only a few dollars above your deductible, you may save future premium dollars by *not* filing.

- **Eliminate duplicate medical coverage.** Don't buy medical coverage in your auto policy if it duplicates coverage already provided in your standard health-insurance policy. When this coverage is purchased, it is usually "courtesy coverage" for passengers in your auto.

- **Don't duplicate towing coverage.** You may already be a member of an auto club and have towing coverage through the club. If so, don't purchase duplicate coverage under your auto insurance.

If You Lease Your Car, Be Sure You Have Gap Insurance

• • • • • • • • • • • • • • • • •

If you have an accident one year into your lease, there'll likely be a big difference between the amount you'll have to pay the dealer and what the insurance company will kick in. *Gap* insurance doesn't cost very much, usually $100-$200 over the life of the lease.

Homeowners Insurance

Your home and its contents may represent the largest single item of your total assets. A loss due to a fire, theft of contents, or any other type of disaster could be a major financial loss to you. Insuring against these losses is important. Some of your contents may be replaceable, while others may represent an irreplaceable loss. You cannot insure against the loss of a family heirloom and its intangible value to you. But you can insure against the loss of things that can be replaced.

There are various forms of homeowners insurance. It is important that you have "replacement cost coverage" as opposed to "loss-of-value coverage." Coverage that replaces on the basis of loss of value will not replace an older item that has little current value. Replacement value will restore what you had before the loss, even though the cost to restore may be greater than the depreciated value of the lost or destroyed item.

Here are some elements to consider for your home insurance:

- **Replacement-value coverage on your home.** Standard policies reimburse losses based on the cash value of your property. Forget what you paid for your house. What you need to insure is the cost to rebuild it. Often that's a wildly different sum.

  A good way to get a ballpark estimate of the cost of rebuilding is to calculate the square footage and multiply it by local building costs per square foot for your type of house. Then add on how much it would cost to replace any extras like central air.

- **Liability.** Most policies come with $100,000 or $300,000 of liability. But unless you have less than that in assets, including your home, it's not nearly enough. If you have $200,000

Give Your Homeowner's Policy a Checkup . . . .

A few smart moves can also mean better coverage for your home and your household possessions, as well as a stronger defense against lawsuits. This example, using rates from State Farm Insurance Company is for a home in the Kansas City area currently insured for $150,000.

Current Annual Premium	$515
• Switch to replacement coverage, instead of actual cash value coverage, on contents	+ 10
• Add $5,000 jewelry floater	+ 18
• Raise liability coverage to $300,000 from $100,000	+12
• Raise deductible to $500 from $250	-90
Revised homeowners premium	$465

Paying insurance premiums for many years without ever collecting a penny in claims is all right. You've gotten exactly what you paid for—a transfer of the risk for certain types of losses.

---

to $500,000 in assets, you need $1 million in liability. It doesn't cost a lot. Today, getting sued for $1 million isn't rare. If you rent, use these same guidelines.

- **Replacement cost on contents.** Most policies only pay the actual cash value on the contents of your home. This would not begin to replace everything.
- **Riders.** Consider separate riders for antiques, jewelry, collectibles, and guns.
- **Floods.** Size up the likelihood of damage from flooding. Check the *National Flood Insurance Program.* Your homeowner's insurance policy does not cover flood damage.
- **Earthquakes.** If you live in an area prone to earthquakes, buy coverage against such a natural disaster.
- **Get a break for making your house safer.** Many insurers reduce premiums by 2% to 10% if you install burglar alarms and dead-bolt locks. There may be another 2% discount for smoke detectors throughout the house.
- **Check on other special discounts.** Some companies lower premiums by 5% to 20% if your home is less than five years old.
- **Unlimited additional living expense.** Most policies limit living expenses while your home is being rebuilt or repaired.

Check how much your policy would pay for special items such as jewelry, furs, coins, cameras, musical instruments, silverware, home computers, guns, and collectibles. Step-up coverage with policy "endorsements" or separate "floater" policies if your holdings are worth more than the basic limits.

Document the contents of your home and put it in a safe place. Using a video camera is an excellent way to do this. You can't collect on a loss if you can't prove that you owned the item. Save receipts or appraisals for high-value items, keep an accurate running inventory, and walk through your home with a camera or video camera to record the contents of bookshelves, drawers, and closets. Keep the inventory in a safe location outside your residence.

Umbrella Liability Insurance

An umbrella liability policy is used to provide additional protection beyond the coverage of your homeowners, automobile, and recreational-vehicle (RVs, boats) policies. The maximum coverage available for these policies may be inadequate to protect your other assets in the event of a major legal judgment against you.

Many umbrella policies also provide coverage for serving on the board of a nonprofit organization. The cost of an umbrella liability policy is usually under $150 annually for a $1,000,000 (the minimum) policy. Umbrella policies will also give you some additional coverages that are not found in your base policies.

Umbrella Liability Tip • • • • • • • • • • • • • • • • • •

You need umbrella liability insurance in case you get sued. Some liability insurance will be included in your homeowners and automobile insurance policies. Being sued can be so devastatingly expensive that you should get an umbrella liability policy that provides at least $1 million of additional coverage.

Your Health-Insurance Options

Health care is a hot topic today. As medical technology has improved, so has the cost of medical treatment. Universal coverage may eventually come. Yet, many of the changes are years away. Focus on the coverage available today.

Become a Shrewd Health-Care Consumer

You can keep health costs down:

- **Get a second opinion for non-emergency surgeries.** Studies show that one out of four second opinions recommends against an operation. Most often considered unnecessary are tonsilectomies, coronary bypasses, gall bladder removals, Caesarean sections, pacemaker surgeries, and joint surgeries.
- **Check your hospital bill.** A General Accounting Office study found overcharges in 99% of all hospital bills. Why does this matter if you have health insurance? Because more and more health plans require you to share hospital costs. Watch for duplicate billings for tests and "phantom" charges for medications that may never have been given to you.
- **Be informed about hospital and doctors fees.** Call your local medical society or consumer-action group, both listed in the Yellow Pages, for price surveys. To get median fees for 7,000 medical services in any U.S. zip code, call 800-383-3434—average cost: $6 a call.
- **Avoid hospital emergency rooms unless it's a real emergency.** Schedule your health care in the physician's office when possible.
- **Buy generic drugs instead of brand names.** Save even more with a mail-in pharmacy.

Cover Your Health Insurance Bases

It is essential that you have adequate catastrophic medical insurance coverage. Health-care strategies for four types of situations are:

- **If you have coverage through an employer.** Many employers offer a traditional fee-for-service indemnity plan, managed-care plan, or both. Your employer may pay 100% of the premiums, or you may be sharing a portion of the costs.

If you pay premiums and tend to incur a number of medical bills, you'll probably save

money going with *managed care.* While your premium may be higher, there is usually no annual
deductible and minimal $5 to $15 out-of-pocket
costs for each doctor visit.

Whatever plan you choose, take advantage of
any wellness programs your company may offer.
Also, use your employers *flexible spending
account (FSA)*, letting you put aside pretax cash
from your paycheck to meet medical expenses.
Health-care reform may knock out FSAs, so use it
while you can.

- **If you buy your own insurance.** Buying your
own health insurance can be costly. Cut your
premium costs by raising
your deductible. Paid
prescriptions and office
visits are nice to have,
but the cost of this coverage is very expensive.
Help defray the addition-
al out-of-pocket expenses
you'll face if you get sick
by banking the savings.

> # *Insurance-Smart Tip*
> • • • • • • • • • • • • • • • •
>
> Solicit comparative quotes on insurance premiums.
> For $15, *Quotesmith* (800-556-9393) will scan 150
> insurers and provide a price list for at least 30 dif-
> ferent policies suited to your needs. (See additional
> insurance sources on pages 139-140.)

You can also shave your health-care expenses by joining an organization that lets you
obtain low group insurance rates. Check into
trade, professional or fraternal associations.
For example, business owners and self-
employed people may be able to pare their costs
30% by joining the *Small Business Service
Bureau* ($125 annual dues; 800-222-5678), a
national insurance-buying coalition.

If you have your own business and are incor-
porated as a "C" corporation, you might consider
a medical reimbursement plan. This will make
all premiums and medical costs tax-deductible
expenses and may save you nearly 50% in
income and employment taxes.

- **If you do not have coverage.** You need to have
basic health care insurance even if it means
scrimping elsewhere in your budget. After all,
one costly illness can wipe you out. Look into a

health maintenance organization (HMO) if you use medical services heavily.

Consider buying an *interim medical policy.* Though rarely advertised, many insurance companies write policies for up to twelve months. These typically have deductibles of at least $500 and often lack the generous benefits commonly attached to company policies.

If you are about to lose your job, investigate extending your benefits for eighteen months by assuming the insurance costs yourself under the federal COBRA rules. Don't automatically take the COBRA coverage, since your employer's policy may not be a bargain. You may be required to pay 102% of the premium.

If you can't get insurance through any other channel, check on *state high-risk* plans available in twenty-eight states. This is insurance of the last resort. You might have to pay $10,000 or more a year for insurance with limited coverage.

- **If you are retired.** Health-care reform will probably improve your coverage but raise your medical costs. But until the changes come, if you're over age sixty-five make sure you have a supplemental private *Medigap* insurance policy to cover bills that *Medicare* doesn't. There are now ten federal standardized Medigap policies available, each with varying amounts of coverage. Make sure you sign up for Medigap around the same time you apply for Medicare.

Guaranteed Enrollment Period for Medigap

You have a six-month window as a new Medicare recipient during which you cannot be turned down for Medigap insurance.

Life Insurance Solutions for Your Family

Getting a handle on life insurance today is a lot like roller-skating on a living room floor covered with marbles. Evaluating policies is often very difficult.

How Much Life Insurance Do You Need?

A. Add up your annual "must pay" expenses (housing, car loans, food, utilities, child care) $ _____

B. Sources of annual income:
Spouse earnings $ _____
Investment income _____
Social Security benefits _____
Survivor benefits from company plans _____
Income from life-insurance proceeds _____

Total $ _____

C. Income shortfall:

Subtract B from A to determine shortfall _____

D. Insurance needs for shortfall (select one):
Assuming an interest rate of 4%, divide additional income by .04 _____

Assuming an interest rate of 5%, divide additional income by .05 _____

Assuming an interest rate of 6%, divide additional income by .06 _____

Assuming an interest rate of 7%, divide additional income by .07 _____

Assuming an interest rate of 8%, divide additional income by .08 _____

E. Additional cash requirements:
Funeral expenses _____
Loans and debts that should be paid _____
Education expenses for children _____

Total $ _____

F. Approximate additional insurance death benefit needed:
Add D and E

Total $ _____

CAUTION: This calculation is merely a starting point to determine your life insurance needs. Is it reasonable to assume that the "must pay" expenses of the surviving spouse will be as high as when you are married? Probably not. Don't forget to factor in anticipated inheritances, also.

Disclosure of insurance-policy fees and commissions is practically non-existent. Finding an agent that is trustworthy *and* an independent source of information on policies requires considerable discernment on your part.

No matter how challenging, the bottom line is: How would your family be affected if you were no longer there to provide an income? One purpose of life insurance is to provide a lump sum that your family can invest or use to live on when you are gone. Life insurance may also be needed to provide for college tuition or reducing debt on a mortgaged home.

How much life insurance do you need? *None*, if you're single with no dependents and you're not concerned about qualifying for insurance at a later date. *Not much*, if you are married and don't have any children. *Plenty*, if you are a parent—especially if you are a single parent or the primary breadwinner. Even stay-at-home parents need coverage if there would be difficulty paying for childcare. Retirees with grown children could possibly do without coverage—unless they're likely to pass more than $600,000 in assets to their heirs and want insurance to pay estate taxes.

The key to buying life insurance is determining how much death benefit you really need. That should be considered before you listen to an insurance agent's (sometimes confusing) sales pitch. Since each family is different, assessing the need is not a simple process.

For an exhaustive insurance needs analysis, try some of the exercises available on computer software programs like, *PC Life Services* or *Managing Your Money*. The worksheet on page 135 will give you a general idea of how much life insurance you need.

Term Insurance

With term insurance, you pay premiums and the insurance company agrees to pay your survivors a death benefit, if you die while the policy is in force. Pure-term policies do not have any cash value or return-of-premium. Term insurance costs typically

Buy a permanent policy with extreme caution—and only if you are absolutely certain to keep it for at least 15 to 20 years (or until death).

rise as you get older. A 35-year-old male, who doesn't smoke, might pay $310 per year for $250,000 of term coverage. By age 55, that policy would cost approximately $1,400.

If you are interested in a term policy, be sure to project costs 5, 10, and 20 years into the contract. You should also know what the maximum charge will be in each case. A policy with the lowest initial premium may cost more (as the policy ages) than a similar policy with a higher initial charge.

When buying term insurance, choose a renewable and convertible-term policy. A renewable policy doesn't require new medical tests to continue coverage in future years. "Convertible" means the policy can be switched any time from term to a permanent policy.

Level-term policies have a set premium for an extended period—such as 10 years. Since the premium is basically an average of the cost for the entire period, you'll pay more in the early years of the policy than with the traditional annual renewable term. Choose level term only if you expect to keep the coverage for half the period.

Typical Annual Costs for $250,000 15-Year Level Term

(nonsmoker/preferred)

Age	MALE	FEMALE
25	$280	$250
35	310	300
45	610	500
55	1,400	900
65	3,500	2,000

Permanent Insurance

With permanent insurance—which includes

whole life, universal life, and variable life—a portion of your annual premium goes into a tax-deferred savings fund known as the *cash-value account.* Your cash value earns interest at a rate determined by the insurer that is generally tied to yields on high-grade long-term bonds. Rates on variable accounts fluctuate with the stock and bond markets.

Unlike term insurance, *permanent premiums* generally don't rise after you buy the policy. The downside: Premiums are four to nine times higher than initial premiums for comparable term contracts (because you're funding the savings account and the commissions are steeper).

People lose thousands of dollars when they drop typical permanent policies after only a few years, because they forfeit hefty sums paid in sales commissions. You are more likely to lose money by dropping a policy early than through the insolvency of the insurer. Surveys have shown over 50% of all permanent life policies are cancelled with 10 years.

Commissions on permanent policies generally run five times higher than those on term policies. With a typical cash-value policy, your agent keeps 55% to 100% of the first year's premium. The company takes another 20% to 45% to cover its other selling expenses. In the 2nd through 10th years, the agent usually gets 5%-8% (or more) of your premiums.

Permanent insurance offers some estate-planning advantages, but the key purpose of life insurance is to protect your family from a loss of income.

Term Versus Permanent Insurance

If any of these statements are true, choose term, not permanent insurance:
- You need insurance for 10-15 years or less.
- You can't afford the cash-value premium for the amount of coverage you need.
- You're not fully funding other tax-deferred savings options such as a 401(k) plan, 403(b) plan, or an IRA.

As for premiums on permanent policies, agents may tell you that you can make them vanish after just five or ten annual payments, by tapping your cash-value account to pay for them. What you may not hear is that this vanishing act will occur **only** if the insurer's expectations for your cash-value growth come true. Make sure that the agent explains how many extra premiums you'll need to pay if your savings account doesn't grow as quickly as projected.

In most states, it's a crime for an agent to return any portion of the commission you pay. But commissions on permanent life insurance are negotiable in California and Florida.

Insurance-Rebating Tip
• • • • • • • • • • • • • • • •

Call your State Insurance Department to find out if insurance premiums may be rebated in your state. California and Florida permit discount insurance agents and other states are considering similar laws. Check with California-based Direct Insurance Services (within California 800-622-3699) and Florida-based Fee-For-Service (800-874-5662).

You don't have to be a California or Florida resident to buy a rebated policy, but you do have to purchase the policy in person. If your policy is large and your first-year premium is $5,000 or more, it just might cover the costs of taking the family to Disneyland or Disneyworld!

Universal Life Insurance

Universal life insurance is a combination of term and whole life—but with considerable flexibility. The policy may begin (and be maintained) at low-term rates. You may need to add more money, to make it work like a whole-life policy.

Interest rate is another, major variable. When interest rates are low, cash value accumulated in the policy is not earning as much as when they are higher. Thus, you may need to add to a universal life contract to keep the policy in force during a longer life span.

One advantage of universal life is the ability to increase (or decrease) policy limits and premiums. This may be done in a single policy instead of buying additional policies, with their separate policy fees.

Low-load Life Insurance

More insurance companies are offering *low-load* insurance. Life insurers spend an average of 160% of a policy's first-year premium on "acquisition

Where To Buy Term Insurance

- **USAA Life** (800-531-8000) sells low-cost term insurance direct to the public.

- **Wholesale Insurance Network** (800-808-5810) and Fee-For-Service (800-874-5602) sell low-load products of several companies.

- **Select Quote** (800-343-1985) is a quotation service that will send you proposals from the highest-rated, lowest-cost companies available.

expenses" (the sales, marketing, and overhead costs of converting you from a prospect into a policyholder). The sales commission is the biggest chunk. When you buy a low-load policy, the acquisition expense is about 30%.

Some low-load policies are sold only through financial planners. You would normally pay the planner a separate fee to analyze your insurance needs. If you do your legwork and feel confident that you understand your insurance needs, you may want to buy directly from the company. See box at left.

As with mutual funds, a low sales fee doesn't guarantee superior long-term results. The real benefit of low-load policies comes if you cancel your cash value policy in the first ten years. You will get a much greater return of your cash values! If you are buying term insurance, shop around. You may find the best rate with a company selling through an independent agent. Companies that sell direct will answer basic questions, but they will not give advice.

First-to Die and Second-to-Die Policies

First-to-die life insurance allows a couple or a group of business partners to purchase a single policy that pays off when the first among them dies.

First-to-die policies are relatively inexpensive. This makes them popular with married couples who work, have kids and want coverage (but don't want to pay for two policies). The sudden loss of either income would be particularly hard on the children. This policy is also beneficial for business partners who need financial protection in the event that one of them dies unexpectedly.

Since your family's insurance needs are likely to change over time, you probably won't keep a first-to-die insurance policy for more than ten or fifteen years. As a result, you should use a *joint mortgage* term policy instead of cash-value life insurance. Compare the cost of a joint policy with individual policies to get the best rates.

Second-to-die insurance is intended as an estate-planning tool for couples with assets exceeding $600,000. This type of policy helps offset estate taxes, and other expenses, due by federal law at the death of the second spouse.

The policy should allow those insured to convert to individual policies without having to requalify. This is important, since your family's insurance needs change over time.

While second-to-die policies may be very appropriate for estate-tax use, don't be overly enamored with the eye-catching premium discounts. Remember, insurers know that (statistically) two people have a longer life expectancy than either has alone.

When to Terminate an Existing Policy and Take Out a New One

If you determine that your life insurer is not as financially strong as you'd like, there are a number of questions to ask yourself before replacing one insurance policy with another.

Changes in your health status may affect your eligibility for a new policy. There are often medical tests that could result in higher premiums or cause you to be denied coverage.

Many life-insurance policies have substantial surrender charges, and new policies usually have high entrance costs. In some cases, you may incur an income-tax liability if you terminate a permanent life-insurance policy. You should check with your tax advisor on this.

When to Switch From Term to Whole Life Insurance

Consider switching from term to permanent coverage when you are saving at least 10% of your income and living on what's left—rather than paying your expenses first and then saving what's left. For most people, this point typically occurs around age 50 (when they've bought all the furniture they'll ever need and the kids have all graduated from college). This also happens to be the time when the cost of term insurance starts increasing at a faster rate.

If you develop health problems, converting to

permanent life insurance from your current term insurance policy makes particular sense. You shouldn't have to pass a medical exam (as you typically would if you were buying a new policy from another company).

The Role of Disability Income Insurance

You are far more likely to become disabled than to die before retirement. Short-term disability income coverage lasting up 1 to 2 years is often provided by employers. What happens if you cannot go back to work after your accident or illness? What will you do for income then?

More homes have been lost due to a disability resulting from serious injury or illness than the death of the income provider. *A family's need for income is even greater during a disability than after death.*

If you are severely enough disabled, you may qualify for disability income from Social Security. This would be the amount you would get if you were age 65 (and retiring). But it is difficult to qualify for this income and there is a six-month waiting period before benefits begin.

The alternative is to carry private disability income insurance designed

---

Disability Insurance Tips
• • • • • • • • • • • • • • • • •

Your disability-income policy should pay out an amount equal to 60% to 70% of your current wages. To keep your premium affordable and assure adequate coverage, you want a policy with these features:

- **The longest waiting period you can afford.** Most policies don't start paying benefits until 90 days from the date the insurer says you became unable to work. But by buying a policy that has a six- or twelve-month waiting period, you can save premiums. Be sure you have enough savings to see you through the waiting period.
- **The right to renew.** This is the only way you can be certain that the insurer won't drop your policy or make it unaffordable to you if you have health problems.
- **Purchased through a group.** You'll get higher benefits for lower premiums. Caution: With a group plan, your employer controls your coverage. Coverage could be reduced or eliminated at any time.
- **Benefits to age 65.** It probably isn't worth paying an extra—25% more if you're 40, for example—to get full life-time benefits. Pay only for coverage until your retirement age, when Social Security and other savings can be your chief income sources.

How Much Disability Income Do You Need?

Here's an easy way to figure out how much disability insurance you need, whether your employer supplies you with coverage or not. (If you are single, or if your spouse does not have any income, simply enter zero where indicated.)

1.   Add up your monthly "must pay" expenses (housing, car loans, food, utilities, child care) $ _____

2.   Subtract any investment income $ _____

3.   Subtotal (Line 1 minus 2) $ _____

4.   Enter monthly long-term disability payments you would get from your employer $ _____

5.   Add spouse's take-home pay $ _____

6.   Subtotal (Line 4 plus 5) $ _____

•   If line 6 is greater than line 3, you probably have adequate coverage. But let's say the number on line 6 is smaller than the one on line 3. Subtract line 6 from line 3. The result is how much additional monthly coverage you should get for yourself.

•   Some two-career couples worry they may both be disabled at the same time. To see if you have enough coverage under those circumstances, add up the long-term disability coverage you get from both of your employers. If the number is smaller than line 3, you might want to get more insurance.

•   Finally, you need to figure out how many months you can afford to live without your salary. This will help you choose the ideal elimination period—-the amount of time before your disability payments kick in.

A.   Enter combined amount from lines 3 and 6 above. $ _____

B.   Subtract any short-term disability benefits provided by your company $ _____

C.   Subtotal $ _____

D.   Enter the amount of your total savings you'd be comfortable spending $ _____

E.   Divide line D by line C (This is the number of months you can get by without long-term disability coverage.)   _____

to replace income which you will lose if you can't work. It is much easier to qualify for a disability-income benefit from private insurance sources than from the government.

Many employers provide short-term disability coverage, (and some provide longer term coverage). Self-employed workers need to purchase their own coverage, unless adequate income-producing assets have been accumulated.

Get a "residual benefit" option that pays a partial amount if you can't earn as much as before the disability or secure coverage that pays as long as you cannot return to your own occupation. Be sure the policy is *renewable* and *noncancelable*, continues until at least age 65, and lets you boost coverage without a physical. Save premiums by stretching out the elimination period—the waiting period for benefits to begin.

Benefits from a policy that are paid by your employer, or purchased with pretax dollars through a cafeteria plan, are fully taxable (just like the salary that is being replaced). But if you buy a policy yourself, the benefits come to you tax-free.

The only time you can consider buying disability insurance and have the chance of getting it, is when you are healthy and don't think you need it.

Who Really Needs a Nursing-Home Policy?

Here are the confusing facts about long-term health care. Nursing-home care costs average $30,000 to $40,000 a year. Medicare pays only 2% of the total nursing-home charges incurred in the U.S. Of all long-term care costs, 49% are paid out-of-pocket. Half of all nursing-home patients are discharged within six months. The length of stay for the other half averages two-and-a-half years.

A 65-year-old has about a 40% chance of spending at least one day in a nursing home, a 25% chance of spending at least a year, and less than a 10%

chance of spending five (or more) years there. In other words, if you're 65, there's slightly more than a 60% chance you'll never collect a dime from a long-term care policy and a 75% chance that you'll need care for less than a year (the cost of which is unlikely to wipe you out).

Medicaid will pay for long-term nursing home care when there are no other resources. Medicaid will not pay for nursing-home costs if you have any assets. You will have to spend **everything** before Medicaid will pay.

Congress has nearly closed loopholes that allowed well-to-do individuals to hide assets. Previously, there was a 30-month waiting period after assets had been transferred to children or to an irrevocable trust, before you could qualify for Medicaid. The waiting period is now 36 months for those who transfer assets to children (for less than fair-market value) and 60 months for those who place their assets in an irrevocable trust.

The most popular way of paying for long-term health care is to provide the funds from savings. But 2.1 million long-term care policies have been sold since 1985.

Insurance companies would like you to believe you save a bundle by buying in your 40s and 50s. Keep in mind that the average age for nursing home admittance is 81 for men and 84 for women. So you might be paying those lower premiums for 40 years before you collect benefits (if you're among the policyholders who ever receive benefits).

You need to take a long look before grabbing your checkbook! A husband and

Should You Buy Nursing-Home Insurance ••••••••••••••••

- **Buy nursing home insurance if:** you don't feel comfortable without the protection of insurance coverage. If you and your spouse are over 65, have a net worth of more than $100,000, excluding your home, and have income of at least $50,000 a year, it may be wise to buy a policy although it is very expensive.

- **Don't buy nursing home insurance if:** you're comfortable in taking a small risk. Forego the insurance and invest the premium money. The odds of your needing a year or more of nursing-home care by the age of 65 are only about one in 33. You will usually come out way ahead to use your investments to cover a nursing home stay (average of less than one year).

wife in their early 60s could pay over $2,500 per year for a policy that provides $3,000 per month coverage. The couple probably won't need coverage for 15-20 years. Some drop such policies after 1-2 years of payment—and lose everything they've spent.

When considering long-term insurance, factor in: Helpful relatives living nearby, disabling illnesses (stroke and Alzheimer's) that run in your family, availability of visiting-nursing agencies, health-care reform (which could result in governmental coverage for home care), and home-care coverage possibilities.

If you are at least 60 years old and buying a long-term care policy, consider the following:

- **Benefit amount.** One way to lower your premiums is to purchase a benefit amount that is slightly lower than the daily cost of nursing-home care. For example, if a nursing home in your area costs $100 per day, you might want to insure yourself for $70 a day and cover the remaining costs out of your income.

- **Benefit period.** Many companies offer lifetime benefits. But with a two-year policy, you have coverage even if you need care for twice as long as the national average.

An Alternative to Nursing-Home Insurance
• • • • • • • • • • • • • • • •

Instead of buying nursing-home insurance—consider purchasing a single premium life insurance policy that permits prepayment of death benefits. Some policies allow you to withdraw 2% per month for nursing-home care and 1% per month for home-health care. Most nursing-home insurance is not needed until you are in your 80s and there are usually no benefits for beneficiaries. With the life insurance policy, you or your beneficiaries will get back at least 100% of your original investment plus some interest. The major portion of your withdrawals are tax-free.

Study Guide Questions

1. How should your desire to trust God be balanced with buying insurance?

2. Name some good ideas to cut insurance costs.

3. List the types of discounts that are often available when buying auto insurance.

4. What types of insurance protection do you need for your home and autos?

5. List some ways you can keep health-care costs down.

6. What are some of the factors which help you determine if you need life insurance?

7. What steps should you take when deciding how much life insurance you need?

8. List the advantages and disadvantages of the different types of life insurance.

9. What are some of the options to consider when looking at disability income policies?

10. What factors should you weigh when deciding whether to buy nursing-home insurance?

"So he called ten of his servants and gave them ten minas. 'Put this money to work,' he said, 'until I come back.'"
Luke 19:13

Your Keys to
Investment Success

▶ Setting Your Investment Goals

▶ Understanding Your Investment Risks

▶ Using the Power of Compounding and Time

▶ Stocks and Bonds for You

▶ Other Investment Vehicles That Make Sense

▶ Investments That Honor God

▶ Strategies for Safety and Success

▶ Investments You Can Do Without

"**W**hat do you see?" The wise old rabbi said to a wealthy friend, as he pointed toward a window. "I see men and women, boys and girls," the industrialist replied, looking through the window. "Now what do you see?" The rabbi asked, as he held a mirror before him. "I see myself." The rabbi replied, "There is glass in the window and the mirror. But the glass of the mirror is covered with silver, and once the silver is added, you cease to see others."

Looking through the mirror of God's Word is far better than fixing your gaze on the silver of this world. He has promised us safe and wise passage through the wilderness of financial planning.

"Trust in the Lord with all your heart and lean not on your own understanding; in all your ways acknowledge him, and he will make your paths straight"
(Proverbs 3:5-6).

It may be wise to examine your motivations before making your investments. Is wealth, power, prestige, or influence your primary motive? Or, are you investing because you want to be a good steward-manager of God's resources? Your attitude will influence your investment choices.

Since no two people are alike, their investment strategies will be as different as their personalities. Actually, an understanding of your individual personality type may be important in choosing a portfolio that "fits."

Wise Investing is Not Gambling

Wise investment of resources, (stocks, bonds, and mutual funds) that God has provided for his steward-managers, is not gambling. In the parable of the "talents" taught by the Lord Jesus Christ (see Luke 19:12-27), He expected them to invest their resources wisely. Obviously, the servants who brought 50% and 100% returns to the master had researched opportunities, sought wise counsel, and diversified their investments. This parable (lesson from life) provides a good model for us today.

"Man must choose whether to be rich in things or in the freedom to use them."
Ivan Illich

Setting Your Investment Goals

Before you begin your investment program, three important steps should be taken:

1. Eliminate all your credit-card debt. Paying off credit-card debt is one sure way to receive a guaranteed, risk-free, high rate of return. Each time you reduce a credit-card balance, the return on your money is equal to the interest charged on that account. You won't find such a risk-free rate of return anywhere else! Pay off credit-card balances (and other consumer loans) before investing funds elsewhere.

2. Build your emergency fund. Use a money-market savings account equal to (at least) 3-6 months after-tax earnings. This is to prevent the forced liquidation of an investment account. What happens if you have unexpected auto-repair bills after you've started investing in your favorite mutual fund? Or, what if the stock market drops and the (paper) value of your mutual fund declines by 30%? If you don't have an emergency fund to cover the unexpected, you have to make a decision: (a) Convert the paper loss of 30% into a "real" loss by selling shares; or (b) Charge the repairs on those credit cards you worked so hard to pay off.

3. Establish long-range goals. The first step in beginning an investment program is determining the Lord's direction. One of the biggest mistakes you can make is not having specific investment goals. Pray about them. Write them down. Share them with your spouse. Share them with other friends. It will help you become more accountable in fol-

---

Keys to Smart Investing
● ● ● ● ● ● ● ● ● ● ● ● ● ● ● ● ●

1. Ask God for guidance as a steward.
2. Start with your financial goals.
3. Select advisors you can trust. Referrals are best.
4. Keep it simple and go slow.
5. Diversify to manage risk.
6. Learn all you can about your investments.
7. Be unemotional about your investments.
8. Don't listen to rumors about investments. Everyone has an opinion.
9. Invest on a regular basis.
10. Allow your returns to compound.
11. Be patient. Invest for the long-term.

You can never take all the risk out of investing. Nothing ventured is still nothing gained.

lowing through with your plan.

Don't confuse "savings" with "investing." If your short-term goal (1-5 years) is to accumulate money for the purchase of an auto or home, then you will need to begin a "savings" plan (using a secure bank savings account or money-market fund). When your goal extends beyond 5 years, then you are "investing."

4. Educate yourself. It's important to understand basic investment concepts. The most basic is not investing in something until you **understand it.** If this means always being limited to insured certificates of deposit, then learn to be "content" with the returns.

Understanding Your Investment Risks

Many investors make the mistake of focusing entirely on a potential rate of return. Equally important is the **level of risk** being taken. All investments have some degree of risk.

The level of risk you are willing to take will directly affect your overall rate of return. *"The greater the potential return—the greater the potential risk."* It's more than an axiom. It's a fact of life!

Risk, for the investor in the '90s, is not so much a loss of principal on a certificate of deposit (CD), for example, but the risk of out-living CD-generated retirement income. With inflation near (or slightly above) 3%, and federal and state taxes generally over 30%, today's CD returns actually produce a negative "real" return.

"Risk" may be defined as the uncertainty about the return on your investment. Review the seven types of risk described on page 152. Then, scrutinize your investments to determine your "exposure."

Progress involves risks. You can't steal second and keep your foot on first base.

There is no "risk-free" savings or investment decision. As you seek to be a wise steward-manager of God's resources, seek His guidance in determining your level of risk tolerance and develop a plan within those comfort levels.

The Risk-Return Relationship

Some investments have a higher yield than others (as compensation for greater risk). You must be willing to take more risk to earn a higher return. Conversely, you must accept lower returns in order to have lower risk. That's why investments like money-market funds have lower, long-term returns than higher-risk investments (such as long-term bonds, stocks, and mutual funds).

High-risk investments will not always produce higher returns. But a low-risk investment rarely produces high returns. Any investment promoting above-average returns, in relation to the level of the investment risk, should be care-

The Many Faces of Risk

The ultimate risk is the potential to lose your money. For example, in an oil-and-gas drilling project, the potential return is significant but so is the chance of losing your money. When you invest, be alert to the seven major risks described below. With proper diversification, you can guard against each:

• **Credit risk.** The company you own stock in can go under or fail to repay the bond principal and interest it owes you.

• **Currency risk.** If you're heavily invested in foreign stocks, your portfolio can lose value if the dollar gets stronger.

• **Interest-rate risk.** The value of bonds—and sometimes stocks—moves in inverse relation to interest rates. If rates rise, and you have to cash out, you lose.

• **Liquidity risk.** Investments such as small-cap stocks, individual municipal bonds and corporate bonds, tend to be illiquid or harder to resell in a pinch.

• **Market risk.** Your portfolio can lose money because of economic or other swings in the stock market as a whole.

• **Prepayment risk.** If interest rates fall, mortgage-backed securities are often paid-off before maturity, forcing you to re-invest at lower rates.

• **Purchasing-power risk.** The risk of not keeping up with inflation may be very destructive to your standard of living. If your investments are earning less than the inflation rate, you will not be able to buy as much in the future as you can today.

Solomon outlined the diversification concept when he said, "Give portions to seven, yes to eight, for you do not know what disaster may come upon the land" (Ecclesiastes 11:2).

---

fully reviewed before you invest.

Remember, *the past is no guarantee of the future.* That's important when you evaluate mutual funds. Most expectations are based on a fund's past performance. On the other hand, past performance, along with reasonable expectations of future performance, is one of the best criteria to use.

Over the past 30 years, stocks have provided returns between 10%-14% annually. Long-term bonds have produced average annual returns between 6%-10%. Money-market funds have averaged between 6%-9%. This shows the "risk-return" trade-off between high-return stocks, medium-risk bonds, and low-risk money-market funds.

Diversify Your Investments

The best returns at a given risk level are achieved if you diversify—being invested in more than one investment category (for example, stocks, bonds, real estate, or cash). It's also important to be diversified within investment categories.

Returns compensate risks, but they do not compensate for all risk. Diversification helps to reduce those risks for which greater returns do not compensate. For example, if you invest in a single bond, as opposed to owning several bonds or even a bond mutual fund, the risk of default is increased. The risk of default is greatly reduced by owning several bonds from different issuers.

You could place all your assets into a savings account, generally considered to be low risk. But it does have one major risk: the loss of purchasing power. These assets will not be able to keep up with inflation over the long term. This inflation risk can be reduced by diversifying into other assets such as common stocks, mutual funds, or bonds.

Remaining invested over different market cycles is a type of diversification often ignored. Remaining invested over long periods of time substantially increases the probability that you will earn your expected return based on the risk assumed.

The stock market offers a good example of time diversification. If you had been invested in the stock market during any 12-month period between 1926-1992, and that was the extent of your investing, you stood a 31% chance of experiencing a negative return.

Being in the market for a five-year period reduces the negative return probability to 25%. A ten-year investment period reduces the negative return probability to 4%. Amazingly, the long-term investor remaining in the market for fifteen years (or longer), greatly reduces the negative probability. *Time significantly adds to your ability to reduce risks.*

Investing Can Be As Simple as 1, 2, 3

- **First,** you decide how you're going to divvy up your portfolio among broad categories like stocks, bonds, money-market instruments, and real estate.

  Here is a simple rule of thumb: The bond portion of your portfolio should roughly equal your age, expressed as a percentage. The remainder should be invested in equities. So if you are 30 years old, you would maintain a 30% bond position and a 70% stock position.

- **Second,** you decide how you want to split your money within each of these categories.

- **Third,** you pick the specific investments to build your desired portfolio.

Using the Power of Compounding and Time

Two common excuses for delaying the start of a savings or investment program are, (1) "I have so little to invest that it won't make any difference." or (2) I'll wait until I can afford it." That makes as much sense as waiting to have children until you can afford ALL their needs.

Example ••••••••••••••••••••••••••••

Sam and Mary are a married couple, both age 25. They decide they want to begin an investment program, but they wait 10 years so they can contribute a larger amount. They actually begin saving $2,000 per year at age 35 and continue that amount until age 65. Their average rate of return over the time period is 8%.

As the chart shows, they would have $606,487 at age 65 if they had began investing at age 25. By waiting those 10 years, they will have only $266,427 at age 65. The real cost of delay: $340,060 ($606,487 minus $266,427).

"The greatest invention of all is compound interest."
Albert Einstein

Starting your investment program earlier has other implications. You may have more freedom for volunteering time to your church, or some other charity in retirement. If your investment program is not sufficient enough to supplement your retirement, however, you may be forced to continue working past age 65 (or find a part-time job to supplement your income).

Cost of Delaying Investing $2,000 Per Year
••••••••••••••••••

Investment started at age	25	35	45	55
Value of investment at age 65	$606,487	$266,427	$108,914	$35,954

Your Time Horizon

Time, not the timing of your investing, is key. Your investment monies should be allocated according to your time horizon. If you are going to need your money in the near future, then money-market instruments (such as certificates of deposit, savings accounts, and money funds) make sense. These investments probably won't make you rich, but there's little or no chance you will lose your money.

The secret to stock market success is time—not timing.

"Time is money," and money is not nearly as valuable without time.

If you plan to invest beyond a couple of years, sticking with certificates of deposit and savings accounts can be a terrible mistake! While these "super-safe investments" may eliminate the risk of losing money over the short-term, they'll make you vulnerable to a potentially greater risk: *The real value of your money will be eaten away by inflation.*

How Safe Are Stocks?

To counter the threat of inflation, you may want to consider a hefty dose of stocks or stock mutual funds (providing you plan to invest for at least 5 years). If "risk" is the possibility of losing money in the short-term, then stocks are EXTREMELY RISKY. However, if you have the tenacity to stick with your stock investments five years (or longer), then your chance of losing money is slim.

Since late in 1925, there have been 64 "rolling" five-year periods. It started with the five years ending December 1930 and concluded with the five years ending December 1993. According to data compiled by Ibbotson Associates, Inc., a Chicago consulting firm, out of those 64 five-year periods, there have been only seven occasions when stocks lost money.

Five of those seven periods occurred before 1942—and four of these were during the Great Depression. Since then, there have only been two five-year stretches when stocks have lost money.

How to Outpace Inflation

Not only are stocks unlikely to lose money over long time periods, they also do a fine job of outpacing inflation. Stocks have returned 10.3% a year since the end of 1925. That compares with 5.2% a year for intermediate-term government bonds and 3.7%

annually for Treasury bills. Inflation, meanwhile, has run at a 3.1% annual rate over the same period.

Stocks have earned 7.2% a year more than inflation since 1925, compared with earnings for intermediate-term government bonds of an annual 2.1% above inflation for the same period.

The Miracle of Compounding

The compounding of interest may be considered the "8th wonder of the world." Building your investment accounts takes time. So, take one step at a time and invest systematically with your goals in mind.

The stellar returns of stocks and other investments can translate into large sums of money because of the way money "compounds" over time. Based on historical figures, and allowing for inflation, it would take just 10 years to double the value of your stock market money.

A day after the largest one-day market correction in October 1987, investors hurriedly called their brokers, "Should we sell our stocks before we lose all our money?" In a moment of panic, seeing their accounts reduced by as much as 30% (on paper), they forgot their long-range goals.

Investors who held their stocks or funds through the crisis, not only regained their 30% (paper) loss but realized significant gains. This demonstrates the importance of focusing on your investment goals and investing on a consistent basis.

Over the years, market timing has been promoted as a method

Want to Double Your Money?
• • • • • • • • • • • • • • • •

How long will it take for your money to double? The Rule of 72 makes it easy to calculate. All you have to do is take an interest rate and divide it into 72. Example: Earning 6% after-tax, money doubles in 12 years (72 divided by 6).

Interest Rate	Years it Takes Money to Double
3%	24.0
4%	18.0
5%	14.4
6%	12.0
7%	10.3
8%	9.0
9%	8.0
10%	7.2

to reduce market risks, protect profits, and preserve principal. But not even the most sophisticated investment professionals have been able to consistently and accurately predict market highs and lows. Don't sell out of fear or buy out of greed. Just keep making investments and let the market take its course (over the long-term).

Stocks and Bonds for You

Individual Stocks

All stocks are not equal. With thousands of company's stocks to choose from, selecting the right individual stock is improbable (if not impossible). Peter Lynch, formerly manager of Fidelity Magellan and author of the best-selling book, *Beating the Street*, said that if he were able to pick 3 to 4 winners out of ten, he could make significant returns for shareholders.

The Cycles of the Economy

A complete business cycle, generally 3 to 5 years, will go through four basic periods:

Prosperity. This is what we saw during most of the 1980s. Interest rates were on the decline, eventually experiencing 20-year lows in 1993. Inflation also declined to 3% to 4% at the end of 1992. At the end of the 1970s, inflation was running 13% to 14%.

During a period of falling interest rates and inflation, primary investments to consider are equities, such as common stocks or equity mutual funds. Try to achieve maximum capital gains during this time period. Small company stocks, commonly referred to as "small cap" stocks, will generally do well during this cycle.

Late-Recovery Stage. As the economy begins to heat up, coming out of the prosperity stage, inflation is on the rise along with a rise in interest rates.

Small cap stocks and funds, as well as those stocks that are considered cyclical in nature, often do well during this stage. As inflation and interest rates are brought under control, the economy enters the third stage of the cycle known as stagflation.

Stagflation. Your primary concern during stagflation is to protect your principal. Cash is king during this stage. Utility stocks are a source of protecting capital and providing a stable income. Energy stocks also serve as a source of protection. The economy begins to slow down at the end of this stage, leading to the fourth economic stage, recession.

Recession. During this stage, you'll want to find guaranteed interest-rate investments, (such as long-term bonds). In the equity market, look for growth stocks and large cap companies. As the economy begins to come out of a recession, the first stage reappears. Prosperity brings with it lower interest rates and lower inflation.

What types of companies do you want to own? Large companies or small? U.S. or international? Are you interested in growth companies, whose primary goal is rapid growth? Or, are you interested in companies who pay large dividends, whose primary goal is to produce a steady stream of income to shareholders (and a secondary goal of increasing value)? These are questions you need to answer if you are searching for that individual, winning stock.

The Dow-Jones Industrial Average (DJIA) is a barometer often used to judge market performance. It is based on 30 of the largest companies in the U.S. When the news reports each day whether the DJIA was up or down, it is reflecting only the change in market value for the composite average of these 30 stocks.

To get a broader view of what is really happening in the U.S. economy, you may want to watch the Standard & Poors (S&P) 500 index. This index is comprised of 500 stocks representing major industry sectors including large New York Stock Exchange (NYSE) stocks. It also includes some major American Exchange (AMEX) and Over the Counter (OTC) stocks. The S & P 500 is a value-weighted index that is comprised of 400 industrial companies, 20 transportation companies, 40 utility companies, and 40 financial companies.

Should you buy individual stocks? If you buy a certain stock, you are buying an equity ownership position in a company, not merely investing in the stock market. Are you willing to take the time to read company financial statements and do the necessary research in order to have enough information to make sound

Discount Brokers

Just a few of the largest discount brokers are:

- **Jack White**
  800-233-3411

- **Bidwell**
  800-547-6337

- **Fidelity**
  800-544-6666

- **Charles Schwab**
  800-435-4000

- **Waterhouse**
  800-934-4410

- **Quick & Reilly**
  800-672-7220

Stock-Smart Investing Tips

- **Don't rush in.** If someone tells you a stock is going to go from $2 to $200, it's fine to tune in nine months later at $8.
- **Don't try to predict the economy, interest rates, or the stock market.** Stick with facts about companies you own.
- **Watch the company behind the stock price.** Don't call a broker three times a day for stock quotes.
- **Be prepared for stock-market declines.** When they happen, add to your stocks and stock mutual funds.

> # If you invest in the stock market, ten years from now you will probably have more money than if you make other investments. The question is, can you endure the ride, which gets pretty bumpy.

decisions? If Peter Lynch, the noted money manager, is only able to pick 3 or 4 winners out of ten, with all of his experience and the support of hundreds of employees around the country, how can you expect to make the right choices? This is why mutual funds are usually the better choice for Christians—acting in our steward-manager role.

Mutual Funds

There comes a point in every saver's life when it is time to venture beyond the bank. Investing directly in stocks and bonds takes more time, money, and expertise than most people have. The solution for more and more armchair investors is mutual funds. A mutual fund is simply a large investment company that collects a pool of dollars from many investors. Individual securities are purchased by the fund in the form of stocks, bonds, or money-market instruments.

You can easily diversify your investments. With some funds, you can invest as little as $25 per month. This also allows you to use "dollar cost averaging." Dollar-cost averaging is investing a fixed dollar amount every period (weekly

---

What You Should Know About Mutual Funds
• • • • • • • • • • • • • • • •

- **No fund performs well all the time.** That's why you should own a variety of funds that use different investment styles.
- **Mutual funds offer convenient international investments.** International stock and bond funds are frequently the only practical way for U.S. investors to invest their money in foreign markets.
- **Mutual funds makes investing easier than it looks.** By making common sense investments in mutual funds, you can "perform with the pros."

or monthly, for example) no matter what is happening in the financial market. This technique reduces the risk of putting your savings in the market at the wrong time.

Choosing a Fund

The first direction to look when seeking a fund is inward. Could you sleep nights, owning shares in a fund that might lose a year's gain in a week? If not, you should stay away from the high-risk fund categories. Keep in mind that in the long run the riskier funds tend to have the higher returns. The trade-off is that such funds also have intervals of miserable performance. The basic fund groups are:

Growth funds. These are the riskiest funds, but they also have the best long-term performances. Growth funds invest in the stocks of companies that the fund manager think will grow in value. They are suitable for investors who can hold shares for at least five years and won't sell in a panic during scary periods (when the value of their investment shrinks).

Total-return funds. This group includes growth and income, equity income, and balanced funds, which invest in a mix of growth stocks, high-dividend stocks, and bonds. As their names suggest, the funds aim to provide steady returns from a combination of capital gains and interest or dividends. This strategy keeps their share prices steadier than those of growth funds but can also dampen their long-term performance. Total-return funds are suitable for people who are investing for a goal five years or more in the future but lack the nerve needed for growth funds.

Income funds. These funds seek to give investors dependable streams of income from bonds (and sometimes from high-dividend stocks such as utilities). The strategy keeps the share prices of most income funds fairly stable. Because the funds offer little prospect for big capital gains, they are best suited for people who want dividend income now (for example, to supplement a pension).

Two types of income funds invest exclusively in bonds: taxable-bond funds and tax-exempt bond funds.

International and global funds. These may aim for growth, income, or total return, depending on their investment approach. International funds invest all of their money in foreign securities. Global funds can invest both in the U.S. and abroad.

Once you've chosen a fund category, you can select a specific fund. Don't buy one purely because it boasts the best return in the past month or year. No investment strategy excels all the time. The top performer one year may wind up on the rocks the next. A better starting point is a fund's performance over at least five years.

Past returns are no guarantee of the future, but past performance is all we have to help us evaluate how a particular fund has performed over a period of time. When you look at a fund's past performance, see if the same manager or management team has been responsible over the time period being reviewed. For example, if manager A has produced an annualized rate of return over the past ten years of 15% but has left the fund, future performance of the fund may suffer.

Finding a Winning Fund
• • • • • • • • • • • • • • • • •

With over 5,000 mutual funds, how do you find the right fund? Several good investment publications and subscription services are available including:

- **Morningstar 500,** a look at the 500 top funds as rated by *Morningstar* (225 West Wacker Drive, Chicago, IL 60606; 800-876-5005; $65 per year).
- **Individual Investor's Guide to No-Load Mutual Funds** ($24.95; 625 N. Michigan Ave., Chicago, IL 60611; 312-280-0170)
- **Donoghue's Mutual Funds Almanac.** Updated annually ($42.95; 290 Eliot St., Ashland, MA 01721; 800-343-5413)

Load Versus No-Load Funds

There are two basic kinds of mutual funds: load and no-load. When you pay a commission to a salesperson, financial planner, or broker, that fee is called a "load." One kind of fund, therefore, is called a load mutual fund because you have to pay a commission to buy it. The other kind of fund, called a no-load fund, is sold directly by the mutual fund company, with no salesperson involved. To buy no-load shares, you call the mutual fund company directly, and it sends you the necessary prospectus and application forms. Sending them back with a check opens your account.

Both load and no-load funds have their roles in the marketplace, and you must decide which is best for

Bank Mutual Funds
• • • • • • • • • • • • • • • • •

In an AARP study of 1,000 customers, fewer than 20% knew bank mutual funds are not insured. Most people buying load mutual funds through a broker or no-loads directly from the mutual fund realize that their investments are not insured. But many people still believe that any products purchased from a bank are federally insured. Remember, as soon as you walk across the lobby and start talking about mutual funds, you aren't at a bank anymore; you're at a brokerage office talking to a sales representative.

your needs. The advantage of a load fund is that you receive professional advice on which fund to choose. Such advice may be worthwhile because it might be difficult for you to isolate the few funds that are best for your situation among the more than 4,500 funds in existence. Ideally, the salesperson helping you will not only tell you when to buy the fund but also when to sell your shares and move your money into a better fund.

The disadvantage of a load fund is that the commission you must pay immediately reduces the amount of money you have at work in the fund. The load can amount to as much as 8.5% of your initial investment (though most funds today charge 3% to 5%). Thus, for every dollar you sink into the fund, only 91.5 cents will earn money if you pay the full 8.5% load. If you pay a 3% load, 97 cents of every dollar will be invested in stocks. In the short term, therefore, you are starting at a disadvantage over a no-load fund (where all of your dollar is at work from the beginning). Over a longer time period, however, if the load fund performs better than the no-load fund, the up-front charge will pale in significance.

Both no-load and load funds levy what is known as a "management fee" every year to compensate them for the services they render. This fee,

Investment Tips for Choosing a Mutual Fund • • • • • • • • • • • • • • • •

1. Choose a fund that matches your tolerance for risk.
2. Use total return rather than current dividend or yield as a measure of performance.
3. Gather information for past performance over a period of three, five, or even ten years.
4. Get professional advice in selecting the right funds to meet your financial objectives.
5. Use municipal-bond funds when your objective is tax-free income.
6. Understand all fees and expenses (including any sales charges). The total cost of a no-load fund may be more than you think.
7. Reinvest all dividends unless you need the income now.
8. Choose a fund that is part of a good family of funds. You will be able to switch funds without additional sales changes.
9. Select funds that have a continuity of good management. Future performance is more dependent on continued good management than on past performance.
10. Use a combination of stock and bond funds for diversification. Or, you may use several different balanced funds that combine stocks and bonds in one fund.

which ranges from as little as .2% of your assets to as much as 6%, is deducted from the value of the fund automatically. The management fee will be listed in the fund's selling literature as part of the expense ratio.

If a U.S. fund has an expense ratio of 1.5% or higher, you may consider selecting another fund. The expense ratio is more important to consider than the load charge (if there is one). A fund's operating expenses are continuous each year. So if your fund has an expense ratio of 2% and another has an expense ratio of .5%, you can readily see that over a long period of time, the 1.5% difference in expenses compounded can make a significant difference in the value of your investment. Expense ratios are often higher for global, international, and speciality funds because of higher business costs.

How Are Your Mutual-Fund Distributions Taxed?

In addition to reporting the gains and losses on the sale of mutual-fund shares, investors in funds must also report taxable distributions made by the fund during the year. There are several types of mutual-fund distributions:

- **Dividend distributions.** This is the dividend or interest income, less expenses, earned by a fund's portfolio holdings.

- **Capital gain distributions.** These are the net profits gained from the sale of portfolio holdings.

    Long-term capital gain distributions are the net realized profits from the sale of stock owned in the mutual fund for more than one year. These gains are taxed at the capital gains tax rate—a maximum of 28%. This is a real tax break if your top tax bracket is above 28%.

    Short-term capital gain distributions are the net realized profits from the sale of stock owned in the portfolio for one year or less. These distributions are taxed at ordinary income rates.

- **Tax-free distributions.** Tax-free funds, which primarily invest in municipal bonds, are designed to provide income that's exempt from federal and, in some cases, state and local taxes.

    Some income funds produce dividend distributions derived in part or wholly from federal obligations such as U.S. Treasury securities. Income from these type of securities is generally free from state and local taxes, but not from federal taxes.

> # *Taxing Mutual-Fund Distributions*
>
> Remember, the separate tax treatment of long- and short-term capital gain distributions applies regardless of how long you own a mutual fund. What's important is the length of time the fund held the security that produced the gain.

Other Investment Vehicles That Make Sense

Tax-Exempt Municipal Bonds

Municipal bonds should be a serious consideration for high-tax-bracket investors. The interest earned on state and municipal government debt is exempt from federal income taxation. States have the option of taxing the interest, but the federal government may not.

The appeal of municipal bonds is easy to understand. For example, the tax-free yield of 6.0% on a long-term municipal bond is equivalent to taxable

Municipal-Bond Buying Tips

- **Maturity.** Hold your bonds until they mature. You won't suffer a loss if a credit downgrade reduces their trading value.
- **Rating.** Invest at least half of your portfolio in bonds rated AAA or AA by *Standard & Poors.* Top-rated issues are less likely to default. Pre-refunded tax-exempts, which are backed by escrow accounts of U.S. Treasuries, are the safest of all.
- **Diversification.** Invest at least half of your portfolio in bonds with maturities of 10 years or less to guard against rising rates.

yields of 9.93% for investors in the 39.6% federal bracket (or 8.33% for those in the 28% bracket). And because the payouts from single-state funds are exempt from state and sometimes local (as well as federal taxes), if you live in the state in which the bonds were issued, such choices can deliver even more appealing after-tax yields.

A lot of municipal bond advertising focuses on "equivalent yields." A 6% municipal bond might be advertised as having an "equivalent taxable yield of 8.79%." This type of advertising isn't all that meaningful and may even be misleading. The ads usually assume the highest tax bracket—and that may or may not be your tax bracket.

Are Municipal Bonds Safe?

Credit risk. Defaults do sometimes occur with municipal bonds. Your money is not guaranteed. Some bond issues are more financially solid than others. "Pre-refunded" municipal bonds, essentially backed by Treasury bonds, are the safest. But their yields are a bit lower than other top-rated bonds.

Among other municipal bonds, the safest are general obligation bonds, backed by a state or local government's taxing power. Revenue bonds are riskier, because they are backed only by the money from a specific housing authority, turnpike, bridge, or hospital.

Interest risk. The longer the maturity (the time period before your money is returned to you), the more interest rate risk you assume.

Defaults. Downturns in a local economy may cause a bond issue to default. Billions of dollars worth of municipal bonds defaulted in the 1980s.

Locally issued bonds may avoid state and local income taxes, but you are exposed to shifts in the local economy.

What Are Some of the Other Tax Aspects of Municipal Bonds?

Possible denial of a deduction of interest on a home-equity line of credit. Check with your tax adviser before mixing home-equity loans with tax-exempt bonds. The IRS could take the position of denying your home-equity interest deductions saying you used the home-equity loans to "carry" tax-exempt bonds.

Senior's tax. Social Security payments to upper-income recipients are partially taxed. Municipal bond interest—even though the interest itself is tax-free—is included in computing income for the purpose of that tax. This can be a difficult calculation, so seek tax counsel from your adviser.

How to Buy and Sell Municipal Bonds

Which bonds do I buy? How good is the collateral, if any? (Some munis are rated by *Moody's* and *Standard & Poors*, but most are not rated.)

To minimize your risks, you may want to choose managed municipal-bond funds. You are investing in a pool of funds with thousands of other investors and a professional is investing in municipal bonds for you. This approach allows the average investor to diversify and reduce risk. Some funds permit an initial investment of $1,000 and additional investments as low as $100. Management fees run about 1%. Some funds will allow the reinvestment of dividends and interest so you can benefit from compounding.

Comparing Tax-Free Bond Yields with Taxable Investments ● ● ● ● ● ● ● ● ● ● ● ● ● ● ●

The following table shows the yield you would have to earn on a comparable taxable investment to generate the same after-tax income a tax-free bond would provide.

If your top federal marginal tax rate is	A tax-exempt yield of		
	4.00%	5.00%	6.00%
	is the equivalent of a taxable yield of		
28%	5.56%	6.94%	8.33%
31%	5.80%	7.25%	8.70%
36%	6.25%	7.81%	9.38%
39.6%	6.62%	8.28%	9.93%

Watchwords of Investing

ASSET ALLOCATION. If you decide to put 30% of your portfolio in bonds, 50% in stocks and 20% in a money-market fund, you've just made an asset-allocation decision. How you allocate your assets is the biggest determinant of your investment returns. For instance, even if you own the best-performing money fund, over time you will never do as well as someone who owns a mediocre stock fund.

ASSET CLASSES. A broadly defined group of assets that share similar characteristics, such as domestic stocks, international stocks, or large company value stocks.

BACK-END LOADS OR SURRENDER CHARGES. A charge from the proceeds of your investment if you sell within 5 to 6 years. For instance, if you sell a mutual fund worth $20,000 with a 5% back-end load, $1,000 will be deducted from your proceeds, and you will receive $19,000. Most funds that have a back-end cost allow growth or up to 12% annually to be withdrawn without cost.

BOND. A bond is an IOU. You lend money to institutions, governments, agencies, and corporations in exchange for bonds issued by the institutions as proof that they owe you money due at some future date. A bondholder usually receives regular interest payments from the issuer of the bonds.

COMPOUNDING. If you earn 10% a year for four years, you don't earn 40%, but 46.4%. The reason: As time goes on, you make money not only on your original investment but also on your earlier gains.

DIVERSIFICATION. This is a fancy word for "don't put all your eggs in one basket." By diversifying, and thus owning several different securities, you avoid the risk that your portfolio will get severely hurt because a single stock or bond turns sour.

EXPENSE RATIO. The total of all annual expenses paid by a mutual fund—including management fees; 12b-1 fees, and legal, custodial, and administrative fees—divided by the value of the fund. The expense ratio does not include any sales fees.

FRONT-END SALES COSTS. A selling commission paid to a broker by the mutual fund and deducted from your initial investment.

GROWTH. This label is applied both to a style of investing and to a type of mutual fund. Growth mutual funds invest for capital gains. They don't necessarily use the growth-stock investment style, which involves buying stocks that have the potential for rapid earnings growth.

INFLATION. A measure of the changing value of your money. If inflation is 3% this year, it means that the value of your dollars will be decreased by 3%.

LIQUIDITY. How easily an investment can be converted to cash. Money-market and savings accounts are very liquid; real estate is not.

MATURITY. The date when a bond issuer repays the principal.

MONEY INSTRUMENTS. Investments that are essentially the same as cash, but earn interest.

MONEY-MARKET MUTUAL FUNDS. Funds that invest in short-term financial instruments such as certificates of deposit and Treasury bills.

Watchwords of Investing *continued*

MUNICIPAL BONDS. Bonds issued by state or local governments. Interest is usually exempt from federal taxes and may also be exempt from state and city taxes for people who buy municipal bonds issued by the state or city in which they live.

MUTUAL FUND. A collection of stocks, bonds, or other securities purchased by a group of investors and managed by a professional investment company.

PORTFOLIO. A combination of securities designed to achieve a specific objective.

PRE-TAX DOLLARS. Earned income on which you have not paid income taxes. Earned income deposited into a company 401(k) is tax-deferred, which means more of your money is earning a return.

RETURN. A measure of how well your investment is doing. It includes income, dividends, and capital appreciation.

RISK. Like beauty, it's in the eye of the beholder. Stocks are considered risky because they can suffer sharp short-term losses in value. But if you're a long-term investor who's concerned about preserving the purchasing power of your money, then stocks aren't nearly as risky as bonds or money funds.

S&P 500. A group of 500 different stocks selected by *Standard & Poors* to represent the performance of common stocks. The stocks comprising the S&P 500 represent the performance of some of the largest companies in the United States that, together, account for more than 75% of the total U.S. stock market.

SECTOR. A portion of the market that shares similar industry characteristics,

such as computer stocks.

STOCKS (EQUITIES). A share of stock represents ownership in a corporation. A corporation is owned by its stockholders (or shareholders), often thousands of people and institutions, each owning a fraction. As a shareholder, you stand to profit when the company makes a profit. You are also legally entitled to a voice in major policy decisions, such as whether to issue additional stock, sell the company to outside buyers, or change the board of directors.

TOTAL RETURN. This is the true return earned by an investor. It reflects not only the "yield" (the dividends and interest you get) but also any change in the price of the security. As high-yield junk-bond investors found out in 1989 and 1990, it's possible to have an investment that has a great yield and an atrocious total return.

TURNOVER. A measure of how frequently a portfolio manager trades stocks or bonds in a mutual fund portfolio; 100% turnover means that the portfolio manager bought and sold 100% of the value of the value of the portfolio during the year. High turnover can mean high capital-gains tax.

12b-1 FEES. Fees charged by a mutual fund to cover marketing and advertising costs, and sometimes sales commissions.

VALUE. Money managers who use the value investing style look for stocks that are cheap based on corporate assets or current earnings. These investors are often contrasted with growth-stock investors.

YIELD. In general, the return earned by an investment.

If you hold an individual bond until it matures, your investment will be returned in full. For the long term, this is an advantage a bond fund does not have. Buy individual bonds only if you expect to hold them until maturity. Otherwise, invest through bond mutual funds and unit trusts.

Investing in Real Estate

The advertising slogan "Buy land—they're not making any more of it" sums up the "can't lose" attitude that many real estate investors had in the 1970s. But as happens with all "perfect" investments at some point, the early 1980s proved that even real estate is subject to sharp downdrafts.

The real estate market has now bottomed out in much of the U.S. The 1986 tax law limited investors' abilities to use real estate as a tax shelter. That caused prices to fall steadily.

The amount of vacant office and warehouse space is beginning to decline. As demand increases, so do rents. This makes some of these properties look better as investments now.

Competitive new properties won't be a problem, since building activity has come to a virtual halt. It will take time for developers to regain the courage and the financing to add new facilities. As a result, existing structures will be the first to generate gains if the market continues to pick up.

What Is Investment Real Estate?

Not your home or your second home. It's property that is built to produce income for its owners. This is primarily apartment houses, office buildings, light industrial buildings, warehouses, and retail space.

Use of Leverage in Buying Real Estate

It is often possible to borrow a major part of the purchase price—often up to 80% to 90%—of real estate. The small down payment and largest amount of the purchase borrowed is usually when the seller is willing to finance the sale.

Leverage is the word used to describe how your relatively small investment of 10% to 20% down can be used to buy a much larger investment. The importance of leverage is that if the value of your real estate goes up, the entire value of the property increases not just your small down payment. For example, let's say you buy a $100,000 property with $10,000 down and the property appreciates in value to $150,000. This is a $50,000 profit on a $10,000 investment—or a 50% return.

But leverage works both ways. If your property decreases in value to $50,000, you've actually lost 500% of your original $10,000 investment.

Rental Real Estate

If you have the time, knowledge, and financial resources, the safest way for you to invest is generally in local property such as a rental house or apartment building. Whether you manage it personally or not, you can oversee its operation and be sure it is properly maintained. Investment in property that is remotely located from your home often brings many management problems.

Investing in income-producing real estate is a long-term project. Real-estate prices tend to be less volatile than more liquid markets such as bonds or stocks. You can use leverage in buying real estate to just about any level that is comfortable for you.

Income-producing real estate is not readily convertible into cash. Occasionally you'll be able to find a buyer in a matter of days, but it is not unusual for properties to remain on the market for months or years.

If you actively manage your property, there are some tax advantages. For example, if you are an active participant in the investment, you can deduct up to $25,000 in losses from other income. This amount diminishes, however, if your annual income is above $100,000. The tax law is very complex in this area.

Raw Land

Investors in raw land are taking a long shot at success. For one thing, vacant land doesn't produce any income while you're waiting for the price to go up. The methods available to finance its purchase aren't nearly as flexible as they are for property with a building on it. You can't depreciate land. All these factors make small parcels of empty land very speculative ventures.

Real Estate Investment Trusts (REITs)

A REIT (rhymes with "street") is a pool of real estate projects or loans, or a combination of both. You can buy shares in a hundred commonly traded REITs the same way you'd buy any stock.

REITs get special tax treatment at the corporate level. REITs are virtually exempt from corporate income taxes, provided they pay shareholders at least 95% of net income each year.

The U.S. probably has enough commercial real estate to last the rest of the century—without anymore building. This makes the likelihood of good returns on REITs dubious.

If You Are Considering Variable Annuities

Variable annuities are mutual funds wrapped inside insurance contracts—the insurance usually consists of a guarantee that your heirs will get back at least what you put in if you should die before withdrawing your investment. Earnings within the annuity compound on a tax-deferred basis. Contributions to variable annuities aren't tax deductible.

While variable annuities can be an important part of building a secure retirement, purchasing them should usually be a permanent commitment on your part. There are significant penalties for early withdrawal of your money. Therefore, use extreme caution if there's even a remote chance that you might tap the annuity before age $59\frac{1}{2}$. Variable annuities are best suited for people in their mid-40s and older.

Tax-deferred annuities are often seen as substitutes for conservative investments such as certificates of deposit or bond mutual funds. As such, they may be appropriate for individuals in low tax brackets. Of course, deductible IRAs also offer this tax-deferral feature.

To succeed in a variable annuity, you need high long-term returns, and that generally means investing in stocks. Bonds are often a poor choice in a variable annuity. Yet a recent study shows that less than 30% of variable-annuity money was invested in U.S. stocks and international equities while the rest was held in bonds, money-market accounts, fixed-rate accounts, and balanced funds.

Here are some of your key considerations before purchasing a variable annuity:

- **Time frame.** The longer you allow your assets to grow on a tax-deferred basis, the more advantageous the variable annuity becomes. This is a *plus* if you are investing for retirement.
- **Convenience.** Annuities take much of the hassle of investing and retirement planning out of your hands.
- **Flexibility.** Outside a variable annuity, you have over 5,000 funds to choose from. Inside a variable annuity, you are often limited to about seven funds (although some funds offer more than 20).
- **Expenses.** Typically, fees amount to about double those for many mutual funds. The higher an annuity's operating expenses, the less likely it is to outperform a comparable but lower-cost no-load mutual fund, even after taxes.
- **Your tax bracket.** The higher your marginal tax rate while your annuity accumulates, the bigger the advantage of its tax deferral. However, if you

Taxes and Variable Annuities

Variable annuities are pure deferrals. You have to earn and pay taxes on the money you invest in these vehicles. The investment build-up in the annuity will be taxed eventually, during your lifetime or at death. The only way for tax deferral to be worthwhile is to have many years of high growth over a long period of time before settling up with the tax-man.

buy an annuity that is primarily invested in aggressive growth stocks, there could be significant capital gains income. This may be counterproductive for high-tax-bracket investors. Capital gains in an annuity, as in a 401(k) or IRA, are taxed at the ordinary income rate (up to 39.6%) when they're withdrawn, not at the lower capital gains (28%) rate.

If you're in a high income-tax bracket, consider municipal bonds and municipal-bond funds, where the income is not just tax-deferred but entirely tax-free. Your effective rate of return could be very similar, but the bonds will not have many of the disadvantages associated with variable annuities.

But if you are over age 65 and facing tax on Social Security benefits, you may want to hold variable annuities because the inside build-up isn't considered income for the purposes of calculating that tax.

- **Payout method.** Many of an annuity's advantages are lost if you accept payment in a lump sum on which taxes are due immediately. The annuity's relative attractiveness is enhanced if you take out money over a period of years. You could draw a regular income—a process that's called "annuitizing" the payout. But, current annuitization rates generally make this a poor option. The payout would be based on a low-interest-rate assumption for life. A better way to take money out of an annuity is to withdraw a percentage or a fixed dollar amount at regular intervals such as monthly, quarterly, or annually.

- **Amounts you may**

When to Buy Variable Annuities

●●●●●●●●●●●●●●●●

- You want tax deferral and are confident you won't need the money for at least 10 years.
- You have exhausted other tax-deferred options, such as 401(k)s, 403(b)s, 457s, IRAs, Keoghs, and SEPs.
- You are in the 28% to 39.6% tax brackets—the higher the better.
- You have shopped around for the best annuity product and found a company that is well-established in the annuity business and highly rated by bureaus like Best's.

invest. Unlike pensions, an unlimited amount of money can be placed in annuities.

- **Surrender charge.** Once you've invested in an annuity and you want to get your money out, there is usually a penalty from 1% to 10% of the cash value. This is called a surrender charge. The best annuities should not have surrender charges after the seventh year and should allow 10% annual withdrawals.

- **Withdrawal penalties.** If you withdraw before age $59\frac{1}{2}$, you'll usually pay a 10% tax penalty on your taxable distribution, in addition to any surrender penalties the insurance company may have. Also, your distributions will be treated as taxable income.

- **Your risk tolerance.** The best investment mix in a variable annuity includes stocks or stock mutual funds. This translates into risk. If you have never bought an equity mutual fund before, or you think stocks and bonds are too risky, then don't buy a variable annuity.

An alternative to a variable annuity may simply be to buy and hold common stocks or mutual funds. Without the shelter of the annuity, your dividends will be taxed, it's true; but appreciation on the value of your mutual fund shares will be taxed only when you take profits (which need not be often particularly if you get into the habit of making your charitable contributions with appreciated securities).

Investments That Honor God

Christians should make investments that are pleasing to the Lord. Would you loan your personal money to a company operating a chain of liquor stores? Would you buy stock in a company that primarily publishes pornographic material? Probably not. But would you purchase shares in a mutual fund that, in turn, invested in businesses engaged in practices that you do not condone?

If you invest in a mutual fund that owns R. J.

Reynolds stock, you might own less than 1-millionth of the stock in R. J. Reynolds or any other objectionable stock. The CD that you own at the bank may contribute to 50 cents of a loan that is made to a local night club. Many Christians feel that this minute interest in an objectionable stock or loan does not qualify as supporting these endeavors.

It is true that boycotting a mutual fund that owns stock in an objectionable company has less impact than avoiding the direct purchase of the company's stock. Even more effective is boycotting the purchase of a company's products in the store.

Although achieving total purity in your investment program may be nearly impossible, you should be able to reduce your concerns in this area by doing a little research. There is a growing segment of the mutual fund industry dedicated to "screening out" investment in companies that operate contrary to their shareholders' world view. This process is called "socially responsible investing." While nearly all of these funds screen out alcohol and tobacco, most seem equally or more concerned with radical environmentalism, animal rights, nuclear power, weapons manufacturers, feminist and homosexual issues, or South Africa.

Looking for a Biblically Based Mutual Fund? • • • • • • • • • • • • • • •

If you want to avoid investing in companies involved in abortion, pornography, alcohol, tobacco, or gambling, consider The Timothy Plan (800-846-7526). This is a relatively new conservative-growth no-load mutual fund (minimum initial investment $1,000).

To our knowledge, only one mutual fund—The Timothy Plan—addresses the moral issues concerning most Christians. Although relatively new on the mutual fund scene, The Timothy Plan is committed to avoid investing in companies that are directly or indirectly involved in abortion or pornography as well as directly involved in alcohol, tobacco, or casino gambling. The fund is assisted in this effort by a number of Christian ministries (such as American Family Association, Life Decisions International, and Pro Vita Advisors) that specialize in monitoring corporate activity in these areas. The goal of the fund is to meet its shareholders' moral convictions without sacrificing investment return opportunities.

If you are interested in additional reading on the subject of biblical and ethical investing for the Christian, try *The Christian's Guide to Wise Investing* by Gary D. Moore and *Sound Mind Investing* by Austin Pryor.

Strategies for Safety and Success

Here are some basic investing strategies that you should know:

- **Government bond funds aren't risk-free.** If you see "government" in a fund's name, you may think the returns are somehow guaranteed. While they are safer than nongovernment funds during periods of rising interest rates, even well-run government bond funds have posted double-digit losses.
- **Fund investment minimums aren't set in stone.** A top-notch, fund group may require a $1,000 or $5,000 minimum. But they will often waive their minimums if you sign up for an automatic investment plan—so that every month at least $50 is withdrawn from your bank account and put directly into a fund.
- **Set up a procedure for fast redemption of your mutual fund shares.** Funds will not mail money to you or wire money to your bank unless authorized to do so in advance. Since you never know how quickly you'll need your money, take precautions when you invest in a fund.

   Set up a wire-redemption privilege. This authorizes the fund to send the proceeds of your sale to your bank. Also open a money-fund account at the mutual-fund group. When you sell your shares, have the proceeds deposited into the account. Then you can write yourself a check.

- **Set a limit on how many mutual funds you will hold.** It's easy to become a mutual-fund "junkie." You read about one fund, so you buy it. Then you read about another fund and you buy it as well. Soon, you own a dozen or more funds. Five to seven funds is usually plenty. Consider owning two small-company stock funds, two large-company stock funds, two international funds, and a bond fund.

- **DRIPs can make good sense.** If you use a buy and hold strategy for shares of stock, consider a dividend-reinvestment plan (DRIPs) which allows you to plow dividends back into shares—generally without any brokerage fees. And in more than 100 such plans, the dividends buy stock at a 3% to 5% discount. You do have to pay tax on your dividends, even if you reinvest them.

  The effect of dividend reinvestment is striking. If you had bought 100 shares of AT&T for $1,950 five years ago and reinvested your dividends, which then provided a 6.2% yield, you would now have nearly 124 shares worth $5,624. Had you spent the income, you would have only your 100 shares worth $4,550.

  Some DRIPs offer a feature that is especially attractive to dollar-cost averagers. These plans let you invest cash in addition to your dividends. That means you can steadily accumulate stock without paying high commissions and without having to buy round lots of 100 shares at a time.

  There are several sources that provide complete listings of companies with dividend-reinvestment plans. Among them: Evergreen Enterprises (P.O. Box 763, Laurel, MD 20725; 301-953-1861; $28.95 a copy) and Moneypaper (1010 Mamaroneck Avenue, Mamoroneck, NY 10543; 914-381-5400; $25 a copy).

- **Look down, not up.** Most people enter an investment by calculating its upside potential and stopping at that point. Look down and calculate your potential downside loss before investing. Using this approach allows you to rationally assess where you should cut your losses—ahead of time.

Investments You Can Do Without

Don't invest in anything you don't fully understand. There's a whole laundry list of things to avoid—from penny stocks to exotic derivatives. For reasons of high cost, lack of liquidity, the size of the risk involved, or the amount of effort required compared with the potential reward, there are many investments you're better off without.

Limited Partnerships

The idea sounds appealing enough. Like mutual funds, limited partnerships pool large sums of money from the smaller contributions of many limited partners who otherwise could not afford to buy office buildings or other high-priced investments.

The fact is that limited partnerships for individual investors with relatively modest assets don't make much economic sense any more. Their major benefit— the ability to pass losses directly through to limited partners in need of a means to shelter other kinds of income—was mostly eliminated by the tax overhaul of 1986.

Commodities Futures

What you trade in the futures markets is not a product but a standard agreement to buy or sell a product at some later date (at the price set when the contract is purchased). You only need to put up as little as 2% to 10% of the value of the underlying commodity

Too Good to Be True •••••••••••••••••

In 1919, an immigrant named Charles Ponzi promised investors a 50% return in 45 days if they would let him invest their money in foreign stamps. He paid off a few investors, thus attracting many more. By the time authorities put him out of business, he had suckered 30,000 people out of $9.5 million.

Mr. Ponzi does not lack for imitators today. Con men, limited only by their fertile imaginations, promote get-rich-quick schemes in every sort of investment, from gold and land to worms and U.S. securities.

If specifics vary, the modus operandi doesn't. Their essential trick is to promise a return that far exceeds the norm, and they are adept at moving from one scheme to the next. There is no sure-fire way of recognizing con artists, but there is one cautionary maxim: *If a deal sounds too good to be true, then it probably is.*

contract to get in on the action. This sort of leverage can lead to fantastic profits if prices move the right way.

The dark side, of course, lies in the direction of a price decline. The futures contract is an obligation to buy or sell the underlying commodity.

Penny Stocks

Many investors figure that it's bound to be easier to score big with a mini-priced issue than with a high-priced one. They have been known to double in less than a week. By the same token, *the biggest percentage losers tend to be low-priced stocks.*

Some investors even believe that cheapness is an indication of good value. This is a false assumption. All else being equal, a $1 stock of a company that earns 10 cents a share is no better value than the $100 stock of a company that earns $10 a share.

Investment Derivatives/Hedge Funds

Investment derivatives are based on such real assets as stocks and bonds, but they work like most professional betting games. They have a zero-sum outcome, always producing a winner and a loser. The bettors put up their money, and a bank, brokerage house or insurance company figures out ways to pass on the risks. These investments have exotic names like *forwards*, *floors*, *caps*, *collars*, *swaps*, and *swaptions*.

Companies use derivatives to hedge against changes in interest rates, foreign-exchange rates, and commodities prices. Mutual funds and pension funds use them to protect their stock and bond investments. But for the average investor, derivative investments need to be left to the professional.

Study Guide Questions

1. What are your personal motivations for investing?

2. What are some of the financial steps you should take before starting an investment program?

3. What levels of risk are you willing to take in relation to potential rates of return?

4. How would you explain the need to diversify your investments?

5. How can you make the power of compounding and time work for you?

6. Explain the difference between a stock and a bond.

7. What are some advantages of mutual funds over buying individual stocks?

8. What are some factors to consider before you decide to buy load or no-load mutual funds?

9. Is it possible for you to invest with relative certainty of biblical values? Are Christians required to do this?

10. What are some investments you should generally avoid buying and why?

Building a Nest
Egg For Retirement

*"In the house
of the wise are
stores of choice
food and oil, but
a foolish man
devours all
he has."*
Proverbs 21:20

▶ How Much Will You Need to Retire?

▶ When to Start Saving for Retirement

▶ How to Keep From Outliving Your Money

▶ Use Tax-Deferred Planning

▶ Investing Your Retirement Accounts

▶ Your Retirement-Income Options

▶ Social Security and Medicare Benefits

Many Christians dream of a secure retirement (especially if they are unable to work) and freedom (to work part-time, start a business, or donate time in Christian work).

But match these dreams with the fact that 39% of U.S. households have no retirement savings at all. The standard of living most people expect during retirement years and what they'll actually be able to afford are very different.

So why don't most people save enough for retirement? Undoubtedly, it is because of current economic pressures and old-fashioned human nature. Retirement saving is viewed as an "extra" rather than an absolute necessity.

Retirement planning is the process of planning your financial future to enjoy a comfortable and worry-free retirement. It includes setting aside money now, in a regular and systematic manner, so that there will be enough money to provide the income you will need at a later time.

Your lifestyle-considerations and intended retirement age are the major factors in calculating the income you will need. Some can live quite comfortably in retirement on a limited income, while others manage to only "scrape" by on a very high income. It is all a matter of lifestyle, spending habits, and your flexibility to adjust to your changing financial conditions.

Retirement is not the only reason you need to build a nest egg for the future. There are also things you cannot anticipate (such as a major illness or the premature death of your spouse).

Saving for retirement is not the same as hoarding and it is never an excuse for cheating God. God honors those who are generous. Are you surprised that those who give generously are often the ones who are better able to save for their future retirement?

Personal circumstances may prohibit productive employment. Often a spouse or other close family members will require personal care. There are many factors that can interrupt employment income

Do not resent growing old—many are denied the privilege.

"The persons hardest to convince they're at retirement age are children at bedtime."
Shanon Fife

for those in their late 50s and 60s.

The Bible does not instruct the Christian to retire to a life of leisure. Retirement from active employment does not mean that you must become inactive or unproductive. Many seniors are actively involved in volunteering and are productive church and community workers well into their 70s, 80s, or even 90s.

They can afford to do this because of their financial planning. Others are able to maintain active and fulfilling employment. For them, it is a choice, not a necessity.

How Much Will You Need to Retire?

Savings for retirement is tough. Figuring out how much you need to save can be even tougher. The first step in planning for retirement is to calculate how much you'll need. Since we are living longer than earlier generations, retirement income and expense projections until age 90 are not unreasonable.

Financial counselors often suggest that you'll probably need 70% to 80% level of your final salary to live comfortably in retirement—and that amount

If you are nearing retirement . . .

- **Review your debts.** Pay off high-interest credit cards. Arrange a home-equity line of credit for emergencies while you're still working. You may have difficulty setting this up once you have retired.
- **Check on your Social Security and company pension benefits.** Unlike Social Security, your company plan probably will not increase every year with inflation. Call 800-772-1213 and request Form 7004 to check on your social security record.
- **Simplify your finances.** Move all your individual retirement accounts to one brokerage firm or mutual-fund company to simplify your paperwork.

- **Calculate how long your savings will last.** If your savings fall short of projected expenses, you may have to take on more investment risk in search of higher returns, postpone retirement, or plan on spending less after you're retired.
- **Use tax shelters wisely.** Use your IRAs and other tax-sheltered accounts for stocks. Put bonds in your taxable accounts. In retirement, take out the minimum each year from your IRAs. Supplement with non-IRA money. Then your IRA savings can continue to grow tax-sheltered.

The standard of living most people *expect* during retirement years and what they'll actually be able to *afford* are very different.

---

will have to rise along with inflation. But living at the 70% to 80% level of their final salary is not realistic for many people—unless they work well past age 65. If they are unable to keep working, their expenses are simply reduced to match their income.

How much you need for retirement depends on your life expectancy and when you plan to retire. If you live many years in retirement, you will need to preserve your capital much longer.

In addition to longevity, inflation must be considered in your planning. If you are going to invest conservatively in government- or tax-free municipal bonds earning about 5%, you will need to save at least twice as much than if you intend to invest in equities (such as growth mutual funds).

As a simple rule of thumb, figure you will need about $250,000 in savings for every $1,000 in monthly income needed, if your funds are invested in CDs (earning 5%). It will take about $150,000 to earn $1,000 monthly in growth mutual funds or corporate bond funds earning at least 8%. Many conservatively managed growth-mutual funds have averaged well above this figure.

Simply decide how much monthly income you will need from your investments and multiply by $250,000 or $150,000 for each $1,000 of monthly income you will need. These calculations do not

Retirement Savings Needed
● ● ● ● ● ● ● ● ● ● ● ● ● ● ● ● ●

This table shows the amount of investment capital needed, earning 5% or 8%, to generate pre-tax monthly income of $1,000 to $4,000.

Pre-tax Monthly Income	Investment Capital Needed to Generate Income	
	5% Return	8% Return
$ 1,000	$ 250,000	$ 150,000
$ 2,000	$ 500,000	$ 300,000
$ 3,000	$ 750,000	$ 450,000
$ 4,000	$1,000,000	$ 600,000

take into account inflation, which has averaged 5.9% over the last 20 years. Social Security and many pensions are indexed each year for inflation with a cost-of-living adjustment (COLA). This will cover part of the increased income you will need.

When to Start Saving for Retirement

The sooner you start planning and saving, the sooner you will start benefiting from the miracle of compound earnings. Put another way, the longer you wait to start saving, the harder it gets. If you wait 10 years before starting to save for retirement, you'll have to save three times as much each month.

Maybe you can't save anything until your children are out of college. But, by the time you are age 40, you will need to have a plan worked out.

If you are getting started on your retirement fund late in the game, trim as much fat out of your budget as possible and double your savings rate. A comfortable retirement means you may have to live frugally now.

What if You Want to Save $250,000 for Retirement but You Get a Late Start? ● ● ● ● ● ● ● ● ● ● ● ● ● ● ● ● ●

Investment Started at Age	Monthly Savings Required at Various Rates of Earnings			
	3%	6%	9%	12%
40	$571	$380	$246	$157
45	775	566	407	289
50	1,120	895	710	559

It's not too late if you start saving for retirement at ages 40, 45, or 50. You can accumulate $250,000 in a tax-deferred account by age 65 if you invest the amounts shown in this table.

How to Keep From Outliving Your Money

Your retirement income may come from several different sources. Included will be: Social Security, employer pensions, profit-sharing plans, thrift plans, 401(k)s, 403(b)s, 457s, employment, deferred compensation, and IRAs (as well as other savings,

The No. 1 fear of many retirees is that they will outlive their assets.

investments, and any potential inheritances). These will vary based on your age at retirement, how long you worked, and the return on your investments.

Not all of these benefits may be immediately available at the time you wish to retire. For example, you may need to use more income from your savings before you begin receiving Social Security benefits. You may also get a higher guaranteed lifetime income by deferring the beginning of a pension income until a later age. Pensions and profit-sharing accounts are totally funded by your employer. Most other accounts are a result of your personal savings.

How Much of Your Income Will Come from Your Personal Savings?

If you have a sizable employer profit-sharing account, monthly pension, or a large inheritance,

How Many Years Will Your Money Last?

Account Earnings Rate	Rate of Withdrawal of Original Capital										
	6%	7%	8%	9%	10%	11%	12%	13%	14%	15%	16%
12%	–	–	–	–	–	–	–	22	17	14	12
11%	–	–	–	–	–	–	23	17	14	12	11
10%	–	–	–	–	–	25	18	15	13	11	10
9%	–	–	–	–	26	20	16	14	12	11	9
8%	–	–	–	28	20	16	14	12	11	9	9
7%	–	–	30	22	17	14	12	11	10	9	8
6%	–	33	23	18	15	13	11	10	9	8	8
5%	36	25	20	16	14	12	11	9	9	8	7

The amount you can afford to withdraw depends on how much you expect your portfolio to earn over time. This table illustrates how long your money will last if you want to take out more than your retirement fund earns. For example, if you withdraw 8% of the original capital each year, and your savings earn 6% on average, your money will last 23 years.

A Financial Snapshot of Your Retirement Resources

Sources of Regular Income
    Social Security benefits $ _____
    Pensions   _____
    Annuities   _____
    Other   _____

Total Monthly Regular Income $ _____

Retirement Assets Held in Tax-Deferred Accounts
    Individual Retirement Accounts $ _____
    Keogh plans   _____
    401(k), 403(b), or 457 plans   _____
    Tax sheltered annuities   _____
    Other   _____

Total Assets Held in Tax-Deferred Accounts   (1) $ _____

Other Assets Available for Retirement
    Money-market funds $ _____
    Certificates of deposit   _____
    Treasury bills   _____
    Common stocks   _____
    Bonds   _____
    Mutual funds   _____
    Real estate investments   _____
    Business interests   _____
    Other   _____

Total Other Assets   (2) $ _____

Total Value of All Assets that Could be
    Used for Retirement Income   (1) + (2) $ _____

The primary home you own is not included in the above summary even though a reverse mortgage on the home could provide additional retirement funds.

You can afford to retire when the income from all your sources exceeds the need for income to meet your lifestyle and living expenses.

you may not need any of your savings to provide monthly income. But if you have not built up a pension or retirement account, you may need to rely heavily on your personal savings.

An average, married, middle-income, male worker retiring in 1994 at age 62, will earn about $1,200 from Social Security together for himself and his wife. Assuming their required retirement income is $3,000 per month, Social Security would provide about 35% of their total income.

Many people born after 1940 will not retire at age 65, but will work as long as their health permits. Their continuing salary means they will not have as much dependency on their savings for retirement.

Dip Into Principal

Most retirees want to live off their investment income and never touch the principal. This sounds smart but it is not possible for many people on fixed incomes. The live-off-the-income-only concept may cause you to overemphasize fixed-income investments, thereby increasing the risk that savings will be eroded by inflation.

A better strategy is building a mix of stocks and bonds, then decide on a set percentage of the portfolio that you will spend each year (regardless of whether your actual rate of return is 2% or 15%). Decide how much you can "nibble" out of savings each year without consuming all your resources. See table on page 187.

Work at Least Part-Time

Look for work—preferably in a field where you

Software Can Help Plan Your Retirement

Each of the following programs will assist in answering the important questions concerning financial security in retirement.

Retirement Planner
$17.50
Vanguard 800-876-1840

Retirement Planning Kit
$15
T. Rowe Price 800-541-1472

Rich & Retired
$60
800-556-7526

Retirement Planner
$15
Fidelity 800-457-1768

Retire ASAP
$99
Calypso Software 800-225-8246

can use your skills. By saving your earnings and allowing them to grow unmolested, you'll have a bigger fund to draw on when you stop working altogether.

Draw Down Taxable Accounts First

Let your tax-deferred accounts grow undisturbed as long as possible. The law requires you to start making annual withdrawals from IRAs, 401(k)s and other tax-deferred accounts once you reach age 70½. Penalties are severe if you don't take out enough: 50% on the amount you should have withdrawn but didn't.

Once you're confident you can make your money last, you'll have earned a significant emotional bonus: being free to make even more gifts to charity and your heirs—without those wrenching nightmares about winding up in the poorhouse.

Use Tax-Deferred Planning

"**S**tart investing $2,000 a year in an IRA when you're 25 and you'll have a million dollars when you're ready to retire." You've seen the ads. But there is a little more to it than that.

IRA's, 401(k)s, 403(b)s, 457s, and other retirement funds are powerful tools for building your retirement funds. Assuming that the growth of a retirement account is over a 30-year period, the after-tax retirement income would be two and one-half times greater by using the retirement account. The chart at the left demonstrates a clear advantage in making tax-deductible contributions and earning money tax-deferred.

The Power of Using a Tax-Deductible IRA • • • • • • • • • • • • • • •

(Growth of $2,000 Annual Contribution)

Years	8%Non-IRA		8% Deductible IRA
10	$16,821	vs	$28,973
20	44,961	vs	91,524
30	92,035	vs	226,567

After-tax monthly income after 30 years would be $405 for the 8% non-IRA and $997 for the 8% IRA assuming 34% federal and state income taxes for all years. This illustrates the power of tax-deferred and tax-deductible investing.

Most people should have an IRA. The tax deduction and tax deferral make this a compelling investment vehicle. You should also have your debt under control and have an emergency fund before you make a long-term commitment of your money. If you have to withdraw from your IRA for an emergency, there is a significant tax penalty.

If your income is too high and you (or your spouse) are part of a company retirement plan, you may not be able to deduct the contributions to your IRA. But it is still may be a good idea.

The tax deduction is just one of the benefits of an IRA. All earnings inside the fund compound tax-deferred until you withdraw your money. If you have contributed the maximum to your 401(k), 403(b), or 457 plan, consider making an IRA contribution. Nondeductible IRA contributions are generally preferable to variable annutiites because of the high fees of annuities.

If you make nondeductible IRA contributions, invest them in separate accounts from your deductible IRA money. This will save massive paperwork headaches when funds are withdrawn at retirement.

A 401(k) plan is normally offered to employees of a business. And yet one-fourth of eligible workers don't participate at all in their 401(k) plans. A 403(b) plan is available for employees of nonprofit organizations such as churches, schools, and hospitals. This is sometimes called a TSA (tax-sheltered annuity). A 457 plan is avail-

Tithing Tax-Deferred Income

When does a Christian tithe tax-deferred income? Let's say you are age 40 and you have $5,000 withheld from your salary this year for contributions to a 401(k) plan. Do you pay the $500 tithe now or do you wait 25 plus years until you withdraw the money during retirement—and pay tithe on the $5,000 plus the earnings?

The most responsible concept is to pay the tithe currently—as you earn it. Otherwise, you will probably have conflicting tithing practices. If you take $5,000 of your salary and invest it in real estate, you would surely pay the $500 tithe currently. So why would your tithe be handled differently if the money goes into a tax-deferred account? Plus—if you don't pay tithe on tax-deferred money currently and your kids inherit the money in the tax-deferred accounts and they don't tithe it—the tithe may never be paid.

able to employees of state and local governments.

Example

Tom earns $40,000 per year and saves $6,000 annually in his 401(k) plan. His employer matches this on a 50% basis, which adds another $3,000 to his account. For the year, Tom has added $9,000 to his retirement savings.

If Tom did not participate in the 401(k) plan but planned to save after-tax money for retirement he would pay State and Federal Income taxes on the $6,000. After paying taxes he would have approximately $4,000 in his retirement account. By using the 401(k) and receiving the employer's 50% matching amount, he has 125% more in his retirement account—the first year alone.

When you change employers, you should transfer the account to a self-directed 401(k), 403(b), or to an IRA rollover account. Use a direct transfer to the new trustee to avoid premature taxes and penalties. You will have many more investment options investing on your own, rather than having just a few options in the new employer's plan.

Once you start saving for retirement, don't be tempted to spend that money. Retirement accounts work only if they remain intact.

You can take money out of your IRA for a 60-day period each year without paying tax or a penalty. If you have to pay taxes and penalties on your IRA withdrawals, you may lose up to 50% in taxes and tax penalties.

Should you take all your money out of retire-

Benefit of Savings in a 401(k) Retirement Plan

	Private Savings After-Tax	401(k) Savings Before-Tax
Taxes Paid	$2,000	0
Amount Invested	$4,000	$6,000
Employers Matching	0	$3,000
Total Retirement Savings in Year 1	$4,000	$9,000

ment accounts because you fear the government may try to take over retirement plan assets? No. If the government wants to seize assets, they will reach far beyond IRAs and other retirement accounts.

If you have one or more IRAs, you must begin to withdraw at least a minimum specified amount, based on IRS actuarial tables, by April 1 of the year following the year you turn age 70$\frac{1}{2}$. There is no law that requires you to spend the withdrawn money. If Federal and other taxes total 40%, you would still have 60% that could be reinvested. If you withdrew a required $10,000 from your $200,000 IRA in the first year, you could still reinvest $6,000 outside of your IRA after taxes. Then the combined total of $196,000 would only need to grow at 2% to restore your total funds to $200,000.

> ## *401(k), 403(b), 457 Retirement-Plan Guidelines* ● ● ● ● ● ● ● ● ● ● ● ● ● ● ● ● ●
>
> 1. Contribute at least to the extent of your employer's matching contributions.
> 2. Invest for growth with a long-term view.
> 3. Do not try to time the market on your own.
> 4. Increase your contributions each year as your salary increases.
> 5. Borrow from your account only in extreme emergencies.
> 6. Repay any loans as soon as possible.

To have the most flexibility, take the lowest required minimum distribution from your IRA. You can always withdraw more as you need it.

So, stop living only for today and make a lifetime commitment to your 401(k), 403(b), or 457 plan. Fund it—or your Keogh, if you are self-employed—to the max. One of the greatest wonders of finance is compound interest. The fortunate retirees will be those who wake up to this fact while they're still young.

Investing Your Retirement Accounts

Many new retirees assume they need to eliminate all investment risk. Instead of hunkering down, keep as much as 40% of your nest egg in stocks or stock funds and the rest in bonds.

Your more conservative investing approach during retirement shouldn't include funds you've set aside for potential heirs—especially young ones, like grandchildren. Those assets should be left in the stock market to maximize their long-term growth.

There are two retirement investing variables: time and the growth rate of your investments. The time remaining before you plan to retire will determine how much time your savings has to grow. How you invest will determine the rate of growth.

A higher return will enable you to reach your goal sooner or require less savings. The longer you can invest also reduces the amount you must save each month to reach your goal. The higher growth rate over a long period of time may result in two to three times more income available to you during retirement.

After retirement, employer-sponsored funds may be transferred from the employer plan. In turn, those funds may be invested in a much broader selection of funds in an IRA rollover account.

Future Income Required
• • • • • • • • • • • • • • • • •

Years	Monthly Income Required
Current	$ 2,500
10	$ 4,072
20	$ 6,633
30	$ 10,804
40	$ 17,600

Based on a current monthly income of $2,500, you will need the income shown above to maintain your purchasing power assuming a 5% inflation rate.

You should continue to keep a large percentage of your retirement holdings in stock investments. An old rule of thumb suggests that the percentage of your investments in equity-based vehicles should be the inverse of your age, subtracted from 100. So, if you're 60 years old, 40% should be in growth vehicles.

Too many retireees convert everything into income-producing investments and forget about the inflation factor. Over long periods of time, you can expect continued inflation—3% to 5%.

Projecting 5% inflation increases your future income needs by approximately 4 times over the next 30 years. Thus, in 30 years it will take $10,804

When your work days end, your financial planning should not.

monthly income to equal the buying power of $2,500 in today's dollars.

Your Pension and Retirement Income

The primary choice facing retiring workers is withdrawing their hard-earned company retirement money in a single "lump sum" or leaving it with the company and receiving it in a guaranteed stream of monthly payments (typically over their lifetime).

If you fancy yourself as a sophisticated investor or have access to trustworthy investment advice, withdrawing the entire company account in one lump sum seems the only way to go.

As long as you have the money transferred directly to an individual retirement account, the full amount may continue to grow tax-deferred in investments of your choice. When you need money to live on, you can cash in some of those IRA investments and pay ordinary income-tax rates on just the money you take out.

You may find that having to figure out how to invest all that money—so it will last a lifetime while providing enough to live on—to be a nightmarish prospect. If so, periodic payments, either over a set amount of time, or for life, may be your best choice.

A joint and survivor option always pays less

Pension Options of a Typical Corporate Retirement Plan
· · · · · · · · · · · · · · · · ·

Comparison of benefits for 60-year-old couple with 30 years' work experience for the male

Income Options	Monthly Amount	
	Worker	Surviving Spouse
Life of retiree only	$2,375	$0
Joint and 50% Survivor	2,175	1,087
Joint and 75% Survivor	2,075	1,556
Joint and 100% Survivor	2,006	2,006

monthly income than the individual option. Most want income to last for the life of either spouse. This could be achieved using a joint and survivor option.

The pension option doesn't leave any inheritance or money for charity. Many retirees in good health are choosing the highest pension option and buying life insurance that will be invested for their survivors' income. If your needs change or your spouse dies, the insurance can be dropped or reduced, increasing the spendable pension income.

Your Retirement Income Options

When you are ready to retire, there are many options for taking retirement income. You can begin taking normal retirement income without tax penalty as early as age $59^1/2$. If you do not need the income, you do not have to begin taking it just because you are retired.

However, you must begin taking money from your retirement accounts, based on your life expectancy, by April 1 in the year after you turn age $70^1/2$. You can include a joint life expectancy of a beneficiary to reduce the amount of the required annual distribution.

Income taxes must be paid on all of the money in the year the money is taken out of your retirement plan (so you don't want to take the money out of your retirement plan until you plan to spend it).

If you are disabled, you can take money from your retirement plan without a tax penalty before age $59^1/2$. There is also a provision for taking money out before age $59^1/2$ by taking substantially equal payments based on your life expectancy. You must continue taking money from the retirement plan on the same basis for at least 5 years and continue beyond age $59^1/2$.

Retirement and Your Home

Instead of maintaining a large house with

Retirement Income Decisions

RETIREMENT INCOME VEHICLE	TYPICAL PAYOUT OPTIONS AT RETIREMENT	DISTRIBUTION RULES AND TAX CONSEQUENCES
Social Security	• Monthly check for life	No required date to begin taking payments; can begin at age 62, but monthly payments are greater the longer you wait (until age 70). A surviving spouse gets an income amount based on either their own earnings record or that of their deceased spouse, whichever is greater. A surviving spouse may begin reduced benefits at age 60—or age 50 if disabled.
Profit Sharing or 401(k) plan from recent employer	• Lump Sum • Rollover to IRA • Deferred payout • Installment	Withdrawals are generally subject to regular income tax (10% tax penalty if under age 59½ unless taken under special income rules); ceiling lowers to age 55 if retiring; 50% penalty if required withdrawals don't begin by age 70½.
Pension from current and former employer	• Pension • Lump sum • Rollover to IRA	May have to begin taking payments at retirement; must begin by age 70½. Payments generally are subject to regular income tax.
IRAs	• Withdrawals (various options) • Annuity • Lump sum	Must begin by age 70½. All deductible contributions and earnings are subject to regular income tax. 10% tax penalty if money is taken out before age 59½ (except under special income rules).
Annuities	• Withdrawals • Annuity or installment	Most accounts allow withdrawals of 10% or more without a surrender cost. Payments are subject to regular income tax and 10% penalty on money taken out before age 59½, except under special income rules.
Nonqualified plans for top executives	• Annuity • Lump Sum	Regular income tax on payouts. Must usually be taken at retirement; some allow a wait of five years or so.

Source: Westbrook Financial Advisers, John Hancock

A Winning Combination
● ● ● ● ● ● ● ● ● ● ● ● ● ● ● ●

Why not plan to have your mortgage paid off by the time you are 55? Sell your home, using the one-time $125,000 capital gains exclusion. Downsize to a smaller home, a condo or an apartment. Invest the tax-free profit from your home for retirement.

several extra bedrooms, find a comfortable, smaller house (or condo). You'll cut your property taxes and other costs—and pocket real-estate profits you've built up over the years. If you're age 55 or older, you can take advantage of the one-time $125,000 capital-gains exclusion on a home sale. Considering all the tax and financial benefits, downsizing your housing prior to or after retiring is often the most responsible approach as steward-managers of God's resources.

It is an excellent goal to have your home paid for before retirement begins. This is especially true if you will have a limited retirement income. If you will have income-producing assets and adequate retirement income, this becomes a matter of choice. If you have a low-interest mortgage and can earn a higher rate of return on your investments, it may be better stewardship to maintain a home mortgage.

A reverse mortgage may also generate needed retirement income. This concept (explained on page 92) allows you to turn home equity into current income.

Social Security and Medicare Benefits

You can probably count on receiving Social Security income during retirement. But if you have a very high standard of living, you should not count on its meeting a significant amount of your monthly income needs. For instance, Social Security may replace 64% of lower-paid workers' wages but only 20% of higher-paid employees' salaries.

The age at which you can collect full Social Security benefits is scheduled to rise. Now, age 65, in 2008, the age of eligibility will rise to age 66. In

2022, it is scheduled to rise to age 67. If Congress keeps "nibbling" at Social Security, the retirement age might be further advanced, all benefits may be taxed, and cost-of-living adjustments may be scaled back (or frozen).

Put Social Security retirement benefits in perspective. If you retire at age 65 this year and have paid in the maximum tax each year since age 21, you have contributed a total of $46,000. Your benefits of $1,147 per month will return every dime you paid in within 41 months. If you live to age 81, your current life expectancy, you'll collect $220,000, not counting future cost-of-living increases.

When You Are Eligible for Full Social Security

Year of Birth	Full Retirement Age
1937 and earlier	65 years
1938	65 years, 2 months
1939	65 years, 4 months
1940	65 years, 6 months
1941	65 years, 8 months
1942	65 years, 10 months
1943-1954	66 years
1955	66 years, 2 months
1956	66 years, 4 months
1957	66 years, 8 months
1959	66 years, 10 months
1960 on	67 years

Social Security may also be an important income source for your spouse and dependent survivors due to your premature death.

When to Start Collecting Social Security

Should you start collecting Social Security at age 62 or age 65? If you're "ready to retire," and you're not planning to work, start collecting when you reach age 62.

Once you begin collecting benefits, you're "locked-in" for a set, yearly sum. Mathematically, the odds are in your favor, if you start collecting at an earlier age. If you begin at age 62 and collect $11,000 in Social Security benefits this year, you'll also collect $11,000 at age 63—and again at age 64. By age 65, you will have pocketed $33,000 plus 33 COLAs (cost-of-living-adjustments). Let's illustrate. If you wait three years, you'll start receiving $13,500 a year in benefits at age 65, plus COLAs. (To simpli-

Social Security Income

• • • • • • • • • • • • • • • • •

Age Beginning SS Income	Monthly Income	
	Based on Average Earnings	Based on Highest Earnings
Age 60 widow (er)	$ 678	$ 820
Age 62	758	918
Age 65	948	1,147
Age 68	1,035	1,253
Age 70	1,098	1,329

The above amounts are what you would receive if you retire today at one of the age levels shown.

fy calculations for the purpose of the example, we're ignoring COLAs). That amounts to an extra $2,500 per year versus the benefits collected at age 62.

Which is better? You can tell by simple calculation. Divide the extra $33,000 you'd get, at age 62 through age 64, by the extra $2,500 you would receive each year from age 65 on. The answer is 13. You would have to live 13 more years, to age 78, to break even. You well may live beyond age 78, but there is no certainty.

There's another factor to consider: Getting an extra $33,000 now is better than collecting that sum over a 13-year period, beginning three years from now. You can use whatever value you want for the cost of money, but the bottom line is that you'll have to live well into your late 70s to come out ahead (if you wait until age 65 to start Social Security benefits).

Medicare Enrollment

It's advisable to sign up for Medicare before you reach age 65. Even if you don't plan to use immediate health-care coverage, you may face a penalty in the form of higher premiums (by failing to register before the deadline).

To Work or Not to Work Past 65

It may pay to work past age 65. For every year you delay retiring, your annual benefits will be increased by a percentage that varies according to the year you were born. The higher benefits will compensate for the fact that you will probably be receiving benefits for a shorter period of time than if you had retired at age 65.

Social Security Earnings Limits. If you work after you retire, and are age 62-64, you can earn up to $7,680 (annually adjusted) without lowering your Social Security benefits. However, you'll lose $1 in benefits for every $2 you earn above that level. This is really a small penalty to pay for the privilege of being active and productive in retirement.

The rules are a bit more liberal for retirees aged 65-69. They can earn up to $10,560 a year without any cut in benefits. They'll lose $1 in benefits for every $3 they earn above that level. Retirees aged 70 and older can earn as much as they like without any cut in benefits.

If you're self-employed, the rules are different. In some cases, Social Security looks at the number of hours you work. They want to see how involved you are in the company. It's a gray area in which the Social Security Administration may demand documentation regarding the extent of your involvement in the business.

Taxing Your Social Security Benefits. If you work after age 65, a portion of your Social Security benefits may be subject to income tax. This is consistent with the original goal of Social Security—a program to replace earnings from employment. If your provisional income (adjusted gross income, plus tax-exempt interest and 50% of your Social Security benefits) exceeds $32,000 (for married persons) 50% to 85% of your Social Security benefits may be taxable.

Working in Retirement— What You Get to Keep

Earnings from a job	$10,000	$20,000	$30,000
Less:			
Federal and state income and Social Security tax	3,015	8,630	12,945
Social Security benefits lost to earnings test	0	3,147	6,480
Additional federal and state income tax on benefits	1,125	1,775	1,775
What you get to keep	$5,860	$6,448	$8,800
Percent of earnings you keep	58.6%	32.2%	29.3%

This table assumes a married couple in their late 60s who receive $25,000 in taxable pension and investment income and $18,000 in Social Security benefits. They file jointly and claim the standard deduction; the state income tax rate is 7.5%.

Social Security and the Christian

Social Security benefits are a sensitive subject—whether the discussion takes place in Congress or between two retirees at the local cafe. The commonly held philosophy is to get all of the Social Security benefits possible from the government whether you are a millionaire or living below the poverty line. It is popular to oppose any taxation of Social Security benefits or reduction of benefits regardless of your income level.

Secular financial counselors often advise: "Why work if you'll lose any Social Security benefits?" Some retirees resort to receiving unreported cash payments for their work (underground economy style) to avoid triggering a loss of any Social Security benefits.

But where should Christians stand on these issues? With God in control of our finances, doesn't He call us to a standard that is decidedly different—one that elevates:

- **Work.** "Six days you shall labor and do all your work" (Exodus 20:9). God doesn't want our lives to be dominated by work but He expects us to excel at it and not be afraid of it whether before or after age 65.
- **Responsibility.** This means not taking money from others (perhaps including Social Security) when you can adequately care for yourself.
- **Stewardship.** This includes investing your money and talents and trusting God for gain.

Is receiving Social Security benefits wrong? Surely not. But receiving the benefits when we do not need them may be getting close to hoarding—which is prohibited for Christians.

To balance the Social Security budget in the U.S., the eligibility age for retirement will probably be delayed beyond what is already on the books. Social Security benefits will likely be subject to even more taxation. Do Christians have a sound basis to oppose such changes? No. Not if our trust is in God and our emphases are work, responsibility, and stewardship.

Study Guide Questions

1. List several reasons it is important for a Christian to plan for retirement.

2. What are several factors to consider when deciding how large a nest egg you need for retirement?

3. What are several steps to take if you do not start investing for retirement until you are 40?

4. List some of the possible sources of retirement income.

5. Name the primary benefits of using tax-deferred accounts for your retirement accounts.

6. What changes should you make in your investment strategy after retirement?

7. Explain the difference between a pension, a profit-sharing account, and an IRA.

8. What are the tax consequences if you take money out of your retirement account before age 59½?

9. How much should you plan to work during your retirement years?

10. What should you consider before deciding when to start collecting Social Security benefits?

Step 9

"Children should not have to save up for their parents, but parents for their children."
2 Corinthians 12:14

Passing The Baton

▶ Where There's a Will . . .

▶ The Myth and Reality of Probate

▶ Are Living Trusts for You?

▶ Using a Durable Power of Attorney

▶ The Importance of a Letter of Instructions

▶ Charitable Planning: A Win-Win Proposition

▶ Lifetime Gifts to Family Members

▶ Why Use a Living Will?

▶ Why Inheritance Planning Is So Important

What you own is called your estate. While you are living you are responsible as a steward/manager for everything you own and control. When you are gone, someone else has this responsibility. Preparing to pass the baton to the next person is called estate planning.

Many people think that drawing up a will is all that is necessary to get their estate and financial affairs in order. Nothing could be further from the truth! Using a will to pass along property could be a very expensive—and vulnerable—way to set up an estate.

It is increasingly difficult to shelter family wealth from the IRS when you die. The $600,000 exemption for estate taxes loses value due to inflation every year. If your wealth grows in dollar terms by 10% a year due to a combination of inflation and real growth, the value of the exemption is cut in half every 7.2 years. In 22 years—if the $600,000 exemption remains in place—your exemption will protect only one-eighth as much of your estate as it does today.

Estate planning requires asking yourself some critical questions. Do you want your spouse to have everything? What if he or she remarries and is pressured to include the children of the new spouse in the distribution of your estate? Or, worse yet, what if your spouse leaves everything to the new spouse and your children are left out entirely? If you own everything jointly, that is exactly what will happen.

Do you want your children treated equally? What about special bequests? What about gifts to charity?

What about the business or farm that is run by one of your children? Would you want them to work for their brothers and sisters or in-laws? Will they ever have a chance to own the business they have worked for their entire lifetime?

> *"We make a living by what we get; we make a life by what we give."*
> Winston Churchill

The Basics of Estate Planning

Your estate plan should usually consist of at least the following three documents:
- A valid and up-to-date will
- A durable power of attorney or living trust
- A letter of instructions

Charitable-Giving Strategy
● ● ● ● ● ● ● ● ● ● ● ● ● ● ● ● ●

With smart planning, you can give thousands of dollars more to the Lord's work than without a plan. When planning your estate, be sure you have at least tithed the appreciation on real estate and other investments. God may have blessed you until you can far surpass the tithe.

A combined strategy of charitable giving, intra-family gifts, and life insurance planning can protect the assets you wish to leave to your heirs from estate tax.

There are many factors to consider, but the two most important are: (1) Whom do you want to have everything when you are gone, and (2) how are you going to accomplish your wishes?

Do you care if a sizable percentage of your estate is lost to estate taxes? This is involuntary "charity."

As a steward-manager of what you own, you will want to minimize taxes and preserve your estate for your family and the Lord's work. The distribution of your estate should be a positive experience for your family.

You may think you haven't done any estate planning. But the way you own your assets and have named beneficiaries for insurance policies and retirement accounts have already set a plan into motion.

Where There's a Will . . .

Since everyone knows the importance of preparing a will, why have so many people never written one? The cost of having a simple will prepared is relatively low—$100 to $200 or so. The time commitment also is not great—perhaps an hour with yourself and the same with a lawyer.

So, why don't most people have wills? Probably because they don't think they need one because they're not wealthy. Others have difficulty facing their own demise—but surely this is not an excuse for the Christian. Because of our steward-manager role in handling God's money, we should be models of preparing and maintaining our wills.

Estate law is a complex and specialized field. This is the reason that many estates are not distributed exactly as the owner intended. Proper planning includes the use of financial advisers and attorneys who can help you set up a plan to accomplish your goals.

If You Do Have a Will—Congratulations!

If you have a will already—congratulations! You are ahead of most people. But you may need a revision to your will if your personal circumstances have changed. Any of the following events should prompt you to call your attorney to see if your will needs revisions: You have married, divorced, had children or become disabled; one of your executors, trustees or guardians is now unwilling or unable to serve; one of your heirs has died or your net worth now tops $600,000 if you are single or $1.2 million if you are married; or you have moved to another state from the one where your will was prepared. Any of these things could affect your will.

> ## Steps in Passing the Baton
> • • • • • • • • • • • • • • • •
>
> 1. Make a list of what you own.
> 2. Determine who would get your assets under your current plan.
> 3. Decide if you want to change your distribution plan and, if so, how to do it.
> 4. Use a legal specialist to prepare the documents.

If You Don't Have a Will

The state will provide an estate plan if you don't provide one of your own. The legal term for dying without a valid will is dying intestate. Do you want the state to divide your inheritance according to their rules or would you like to decide how it's split? Do you want a court to decide about the supervision of your minor children? Would you want your children to receive their entire inheritance at soon as age 18—as would happen in many states? The outcome may be very different from what you would want—plus be very expensive.

When a Christian dies without a valid will, or other legal estate planning instrument, it leaves important decisions to a secular judicial system. While you would not do this by choice, it is done by default if you do not make the proper plans and preparation.

The probate process only relates to the costs and time involved in settling an estate—and nothing to do with potential tax liability.

What is the most common problem with estate planning? Failure to make a plan that accomplishes one's objectives. Through a lack of information or having the wrong information, many make provisions that do something totally different from what they really wanted.

The Myth and Reality of Probate

Even if you have a will, some or all of your assets must go through a court procedure called probate. The court determines if your will is valid. Your property is inventoried and appraised, and your creditors are paid. When all these conditions are met, your estate may be distributed to your heirs.

You may be attracted to alternatives to probate in a desire to handle the estate distribution process faster, cheaper, and more privately than through a probate court. It is possible to by-pass probate, but it takes a great deal of planning and thorough comprehension of estate-planning rules.

Don't Confuse Probate With Estate Taxes • • • • • • • • • • • • • • •

The probate process does not generate any revenue to the state or federal government in the form of taxes. But there are legal fees and expenses involved.

Estate taxes, on the other hand, are based on who had ownership and control of the property, regardless of whether that property goes through probate.

Advantages of probate
- **Claims by creditors.** When an estate has been

probated and its assets distributed, no creditor can make a claim against the assets.

- **Separate entity.** An estate is a separate taxable entity. This may provide opportunities to reduce taxes by shifting income to an heir or keeping it in the estate a bit longer if the estate's tax bracket is lower than the heir's.
- **Expense.** It usually costs less for an attorney to draft a will than to draft a living trust.

Disadvantages of probate

- **Probate is expensive.** It is a court process that involves lawyers. This is the greatest expense in the probate process—averaging 3% to 5% of an estate's gross value.
- **Probate is time consuming.** The process normally takes a minimum of nine months up to several years to complete, delaying the ultimate distribution of assets. Delays can result from claims of creditors, disagreements between heirs, problems in proving ownership of assets, and normal delays in the legal process.
- **Probate is a public process.** Probate records are open to the public and anyone can read a will that has been filed.

If you desire to side-step much of the probate process, one of the techniques most frequently used is a revocable living trust.

Are Living Trusts for You?

A revocable living trust allows you to carry probate avoidance to the highest level. Simply stated, it is a strategy of giving your assets to a trust so the assets are out of your name. The trust allows you a change of heart later on if you so choose. But if you don't it snaps shut at the instant of your death, and essentially you die owning little or no probate property.

This technique is called the revocable living trust—*revocable* because you are able to change your mind later if your circumstances or attitudes change and *living* because you create the trust while you are alive.

Some of the key aspects of a revocable living trust are:

- **Probate costs saved.** Most of the probate costs discussed on page 209 can be saved.
- **Title to assets.** The process of retitling all of your assets may be very time consuming. It may involve stock brokerage firms, transfer agents, mutual fund companies, and banks.
- **Time savings.** Months or even years can be saved as compared to having all your assets go through the probate process.
- **The trust must be funded.** This means that title to your assets must be transferred to the trust. If all of your assets (with certain exceptions, for example, such as your car, personal effects, and furniture) are not transferred to the trust, your trust will not work as you intended.
- **Flexibility.** Revocable living trusts are very flexible. For example, the trust can be named as beneficiary of your insurance policies and other assets that provide you the opportunity to designate a beneficiary.
- **A will is still needed.** A revocable living trust is not a substitute for a will. Since assets often get inadvertently or intentionally left out of the trust, you still need a "pour-over" will that transfers all assets to the trust through probate.
- **No tax savings.** Contrary to popular belief, and to what some promoters would have you believe, a living trust does not avoid inheritance or federal estate taxes. It is simply not a tax-savings device. Nothing can be done through a revocable living trust to save taxes that can't be done with a properly drafted will.

When Living Trusts Make Sense

You need a will in all 50 states. A living trust may be a good idea when:

- You own property in more than one state
- You have a high risk of becoming incapacitated
- You want to keep the terms of your trust private
- You're worried about a will being contested
- You are in a second marriage

- **Expense to set-up.** Up-front expenses typically start at $1,000 just to prepare the trust documents, and many trusts cost more. If you use an outside administrator, such as a bank, you'll pay a percentage of your trust assets each year for that service.

Not everyone should worry about probate. Depending on the size of your estate, the state laws where you reside, and other factors, probate may be the best alternative. If a competent family member is executor of your estate, working with a skilled and honest lawyer, the difficulties of the probate process can be kept to a minimum.

Who should consider using a revocable living trust? Anyone who has any substantial amount of assets should at least consider it. It may make the most sense for people who own property in several states (and don't want to pay probate costs in each of them), elderly single people whose children or heirs do not live nearby, and those whose children may disagree over the estate distribution.

If you are not certain whether you need a living trust, seek out an attorney to answer your questions. Probate avoidance is not lawyer avoidance.

Using a Durable Power of Attorney

An accident, illness, or just plain aging may leave you incapacitated. If you are unable to handle your own affairs, a court order may revoke your right to manage your own money. If so, they will appoint a guardian or conservator—but it may not be the one you would have chosen.

The simplest way to protect yourself—and to ensure that your property will continue to be managed as you see fit—is to appoint a guardian for yourself through a durable power of attorney. If you ever become unable to manage your own financial and personal affairs, someone you trust will be able to act on your behalf.

A general power of attorney gives the named individual virtually limitless control over your affairs. This is often not necessary. You may use special powers of attorney to give different people responsibility for different matters. You may want one person to manage your finances and another to make decisions regarding your health care and housing.

A power of attorney may be indefinite (durable) or for a specific period of time. Either way, it may be canceled at any time, and it terminates immediately upon your death.

The Importance of a Letter of Instructions

Your will and durable power of attorney are more important than a letter of instructions. If you decide to make a living will or living trust, they are probably more important also. But a letter of instructions will save your loved ones needless worry and frustration.

A letter of instructions is not a legal document like a will. You have a lot more leeway in both its language and contents. It is a good place to put personal wishes and final comments. But the more important use of a letter is to provide specific information about matters such as:

- Funeral home arrangements
- Vital statistics to give to the funeral director
- Location of insurance policies
- Attorney's name and telephone number
- Broker's name and telephone number
- Expected death benefits from employer, Social Security, Veteran's Administration, or other sources
- A list of who is to receive certain personal effects
- Location of your will and other important personal papers
- Location of safety deposit box and key
- Location of income tax return files

- Information on loans outstanding
- Life insurance and other policy information
- Data on investments

A well-prepared letter of instructions is a wonderful way to organize your records. But keep it up-to-date, since this information will frequently change. And don't forget to let your family members know where the letter is!

Charitable Planning: A Win-Win Proposition

There are a variety of charitable-planning techniques for generous people. Consider some of these concepts to provide for your church and other charities while avoiding income or estate taxes.

Charitable Remainder Trusts

A charitable-remainder trust may be used to make future gifts to charity and provide current or future income to you and to other beneficiaries.

Here's how it works: You place assets that will pass to a charity at a future date (or upon your death) in a trust. You retain an income flow from the assets. You also get an income-tax deduction now for the value of the gift that will pass to the charity when you die. If you give appreciated property, you avoid paying capital-gains tax.

You must elect to take an annual percentage payout from the trust, such as 6%. The trust is tax-exempt, so investment earnings compound tax-free. You can be the trustee of the trust and control its investments.

The trust assets grow tax-deferred. Taxes are paid by the beneficiaries, based on the type of income earned by the trust.

Charitable-remainder trusts are irrevocable. While you may change the charitable beneficiary, you cannot withdraw contributions to the trust.

Contributions to a charitable trust are not subject to the dollar limits that apply to other retirement contributions—such as the $2,000 annual IRA limit or the annual limit for 401(k), 403(b), or 457 plans.

Example •

Joe and Mary are in their mid-60s. Their estate is valued at $1,500,000. Included in their estate is stock they bought for $50,000. It is now worth $600,000. If they sell the stock, the income taxes would be over $217,000. This would leave them only $383,000 to invest. If they earn 8% on the $383,000, their pre-tax income would be $30,640.

They would like to make a generous gift to their church. They decide to set up a charitable-remainder trust and make a gift of the stock to the trust. If the trust sells the stock, there is no income tax on the gain. If the trust earns 8% on the $600,000 and they chose an 8% payout rate, they would have pre-tax income of $48,000— $17,360 more than if they sold the stock themselves. They also have an income-tax deduction based on the value of the gift.

A charitable trust may also be the beneficiary of IRAs and other retirement funds. Life insurance is free from estate tax if it is placed in a charitable-remainder unitrust. You can use the current tax savings and increased income derived from the trust to buy life insurance that will pay your heirs an amount equal to what they would have received after taxes from your estate.

Property given to a charitable-remainder unitrust ultimately goes to the Lord's work instead of to your heirs. Assets transferred to a trust are removed from your estate, so the estate will pay less estate tax. The assets in the trust will also avoid probate.

There are two types of charitable-remainder trusts:

• **Charitable-remainder unitrust.** You give the assets to the charity, which then pays you or you

By planning your giving, you can make the gifts you have long wanted to give but thought you could not afford.

and your spouse a fixed percentage (5%-12%) of the fund until death or a specified date. At that time, the principal goes to the charity. If the money is invested properly, it will grow and you'll be getting a fixed percentage of a greater sum. This makes this type of trust a good hedge against inflation.

- **Charitable-remainder annuity trust.** Here, the donor receives a fixed dollar amount from the trust every year for life or a fixed number of years, regardless of how well—or how poorly—the assets are managed by the trustee. This guarantees a fixed stream of income that you may find comforting.

These charitable vehicles require the assistance of a professional adviser who is familiar with estate planning and the tax law. Even though the tax savings may make giving very attractive, there should still be a basic motivation to give to the charity. In most charitable giving arrangements, a donor is still generally giving up the right to get the principal back.

Benefits of a Charitable-Remainder Trust
● ● ● ● ● ● ● ● ● ● ● ● ● ●

1. A current charitable-contribution deduction.
2. No capital gains taxes on the sale of your property.
3. No estate taxes on your trust's assets.
4. Lifetime income from the assets.
5. Future control over charitable gifts.

Check with your favorite charity or organization about their charitable trust arrangements. If you do not need lifetime income, consider a "gift trust" for an individual or charity through a mutual fund family: **Twentieth Century Investors Gift Trust** (800-345-2021; $250 minimum) and **Fidelity Investors** (800-544-0275; $10,000 minimum).

Charitable-Gift Annuities
You can transfer cash or assets to your church

Comparison of Charitable Contribution Techniques

Type of Gift	Form of Gift	Advantages	Disadvantages
Outright Gifts	Cash Securities Real estate Existing life-insurance policies	• 100% deductible for income tax	• No retained interest
Bequests	Anything owned at time of death	• Retains control during lifetime and distributes as desired at death	• No income tax deduction
Charitable Lead Trust	Cash Securities Real estate Closely-held business	• Allows property to transfer to heirs with little or no estate tax	• No real income-tax advantage
Pooled Income Fund	Cash Appreciated securities	• Portion deductible for income tax • Potential inflation hedge • No capital gains tax on appreciated securities	• Donor cannot be the trustee • Not available from all charitable organizations
Charitable-Remainder Unitrust	Cash Real estate Appreciated securities	• Portion deductible for income tax • No capital gains tax on appreciated property • Potential inflation hedge	• Income will decline if the value of the fund declines

Comparison of Charitable Contribution Techniques *continued*

Type of Gift	Form of Gift	Advantages	Disadvantages
Charitable-Remainder Annuity Trust	Cash Appreciated securities	• Portion deductible for income tax • No capital gains tax on appreciated property • Fixed income	• Income is fixed, regardless of need or inflation
Gift of Insurance (Charity is owner and beneficiary)	Existing policies New policies in certain states	• Income tax deduction for value of policy • Premium payments may be deducted as gift • Enables donor to make large future gift at small cost	• May require annual premiums
Charitable - Gift Annuity	Cash Appreciated securities	• Guaranteed payments for life • Portion deductible for income tax • Portion of annual payments are income-tax free	• Income is fixed, regardless of need or inflation
Life Estate	Personal residence or farm	• Life use of the property • Portion deductible for income tax	• May face capital-gains taxes
Revocable Charitable Trust	Cash Securities Real estate	• Avoids work and worry of investment management • Trust assets available if needed	• No income-tax deduction

or other charity in exchange for a charitable-gift annuity. Payments are made at least annually to one or two "annuitants." The annuitants are usually you and your spouse.

The advantages of charitable-gift annuities are several:

- You receive regular payments for as long as you live.
- The payments are legally guaranteed by the church or nonprofit organization.
- Part of each payment may be exempt from income taxes.
- You may claim the present value of your gift as a charitable deduction.
- You may use charitable-gift annuities as retirement income plans. For example, you may elect not to receive payments until ten years after you make the gifts. This is a deferred-gift annuity and it pays higher rates than immediate-gift annuities.

Life Estates

If you give your personal residence or farm to your church or other charity, you may stipulate that you or other people may continue to use the property as long as you or they live. After your death, or the death of the people named to use the property, the charity gets total control of the property.

Your advantages of this type of gift include:

- You can use the residence or farm as long as you live.
- You usually may take an immediate deduction of the present value for income-tax purposes.
- Your estate is reduced by the gift.

Revocable Charitable Trusts

A revocable trust is simply what its name implies—if you are the one setting up a revocable trust, you can revoke it. At your passing, the trust then becomes irrevocable. The trust can become irrevocable sooner if you give up your power to revoke it.

A revocable trust is an excellent tool to use when you want to get the paperwork lined up for a gift to your favorite charity but you are not quite ready to release ownership of the asset.

It provides you the following benefits:

- You have complete control over the trust assets as long as you live.
- The trust is relatively simple to set up.
- The trust assets are not subject to probate at your passing.

Lifetime Gifts to Family Members

Lifetime giving is an important way to share God's blessing and to emphasize your priorities. You can also cut estate taxes by giving property away to your family during your lifetime, thereby reducing the size of your taxable estate. But when you give property away, you must be concerned with gift taxes.

You can give up to $10,000 a year to each of any number of individuals without having to pay federal gift tax. A husband and wife can join together to make gifts of $20,000 annually. These are personal gifts and they do not qualify as charitable deductions.

This is an annual tax break. If you don't use it, you lose it. Of course, more could be given to any individual in any one year. Any amount more than $10,000 that you individually give to one donee simply requires the filing of a gift-tax return. This has the effect of using a portion of your $600,000 lifetime estate-tax exclusion.

In addition to the $10,000/$20,000 amounts, payments made directly to an institution or caregiver for a person's current education or medical care are free from gift tax. There is no limit on the amount. **Caution:** The payment cannot be given directly to the person who benefits from the payment to qualify under the gift tax exclusion.

Before giving away property, consider using income-tax strategies. If you have a loss on a property, sell it, take the loss, and give the proceeds. This preserves your capital-loss deduction. If you have a gain on a property, you have a choice of giving the property or selling it and then giving the proceeds. Your choice will depend on the tax bracket of the beneficiary and whether you want to pass the tax burden on to the beneficiary.

You may want to assist your children or other relatives in paying college expenses. These gifts reduce your taxable estate and are a wise way to avoid unnecessary estate taxes.

Life Insurance Trusts

Smart use of second-to-die insurance (see page 140) may enable you to pass on a multiple of the $600,000 estate tax-exemption amount free of estate tax. This policy will pay the estate tax upon the death of the second spouse. Second-to-die insurance is cheaper than those that pay off when one person dies—and it solves the problem of covering what could be a heavy tax bill because the marital deduction can no longer be utilized.

Use of an irrevocable life-insurance trust to own, as well as receive, the proceeds of a policy can also eliminate all estate taxes on the proceeds (if the insurance policy is purchased by the trust). Under current estate tax laws, this could save as much as 60% on estate taxes for the death benefit. This makes wise planning very important.

Life-insurance trusts are irrevocable and must meet technical requirements to be free of estate tax. This is not a do-it-yourself project. Consult your attorney.

Why Use a Living Will?

Advances in medical care have produced many miracles. Illnesses that were invariably fatal to earlier generations are now curable. This progress has not been without unpleasant side effects. For example, it is now possible to sustain life well beyond the point at which there is any apparent chance for recovery. Patients who are in irreversible comas or the final stages of terminal illness can be fed through tubes. Their hearts and lungs can be kept functioning by mechanical devices. Their lives can be prolonged for years.

A living will is often confused with a living trust. It is used independently of a will or living trust.

A living will, sometimes called "advance directives," is a written instruction that tells doctors whether you want extreme measures taken to keep you alive during a terminal illness. Without such guidance, doctors generally must use all means possible to sustain life.

A living will is not always adhered to by hospitals and some states don't recognize it. However, it still may be better to leave such instructions than to have nothing at all. Give copies of your living will to your lawyer, clergyman, and the person to whom you give your power of attorney. The living will can be easily revoked at any time.

Most states have adopted uniform regulations for living wills. A lawyer might charge $50 to $150 for a living will.

While not all Christians agree on the use of a living will, occasions will arise when crucial medical decisions must be made. Family members may be called upon to make choices on continuing aggressive medical treatment or limiting the use of life-sustaining procedures when illness or injury is determined to be terminal. Prayerfully considering the medical treatment you wish in such an

Consider a Durable Power of Attorney for Health

Living wills have limitations. Doctors may be unable to honor your wishes because the language in your living will is either too specific or too general. The solution? Prepare another document—a durable power of attorney for health. (This is distinct from a general power of attorney described on page 211 which deals with finances.) Designate a close family member or friend to make medical decisions for you after doctors have determined that you are unable to do so.

Use the living will as a backup to your durable power of attorney for health. Word it so that the living will goes into effect only when your health care agent can't be reached. If you spend part of the year in another state (for example, winter in Florida), you may need to draw up a separate living will and durable power of attorney for health in each state.

Sample Revocable Living Will

If I am not able to make an informed decision regarding my health care, I direct my health care-providers to follow my instructions as set forth below. (Initial those statements you wish to be included in the document and cross through those statements that do not apply.)

A. If my death from a terminal condition is imminent, and even if life-sustaining procedures are used, there is no reasonable expectation of my recovery:

_____ I direct that my life not be extended by life-sustaining procedures, including the administration of nutrition and hydration artificially.

_____ I direct that my life not be extended by life-sustaining procedures, except that, if I am unable to take food by mouth, I wish to receive nutrition and hydration artificially.

_____ I direct that, even in a terminal condition, I be given all available medical treatment in accordance with accepted health-care standards.

B. If I am in a persistent vegetative state, that is, if I am not conscious and am not aware of my environment nor able to interact with others, and there is no reasonable expectation of my recovery within a medically appropriate period:

_____ I direct that my life not be extended by life-sustaining procedures, including the administration of nutrition and hydration artificially.

_____ I direct that my life not be extended by life-sustaining procedures, except that if I am unable to take in food by mouth, I wish to receive nutrition and hydration artificially.

_____ I direct that I be given all available medical treatment in accordance with accepted health-care standards.

C. If I am pregnant, my agent shall follow these specific instructions:

By signing below, I indicate that I am emotionally and mentally competent to make the Revocable Living Will and that I understand its purpose and effect.

_____   _____
(Date)   (Signature of Declarant)

The Declarant signed or acknowledged signing this revocable living will in my presence, and based upon my personal observation, the Declarant appears to be a competent individual.

_____   _____
(Witness)   (Witness)

Caution: The form of revocable living wills varies based on state law. To receive free copies of forms for creating a revocable living will and durable power of attorney for health in your state, with instructions, call 800-989-9455.

event—and expressing those wishes to your loved ones—may alleviate difficult decisions by family members.

Certainly, life is precious in God's eyes—both born and unborn. "For you created my inmost being; you knit me together in my mother's womb. I praise you because I am fearfully and wonderfully made" (Psalm 139:13-14).

Why Inheritance Planning Is So Important

Two of the biggest mistakes commonly made by heirs are: Out of fear of offending their parents, they remain too passive about the inheritance process. That sets the stage for trouble later on.

Ideally, your parents should bring up the subject. If they don't and your parents have a taxable estate, ask if they have done tax planning to reduce their estate taxes. They may need professional help but be reluctant to seek advice or not know what they should do.

The second mistake is acting too quickly right after an inheritance. When heirs receive a sudden windfall, they're besieged by people selling a variety of investments. Instead of making a fast decision about how to invest, they should put the money in something safe and liquid—like a money market account—until they have formed a long-term game plan.

> ## *Your Estate-Tax Exclusion*
> • • • • • • • • • • • • • • • • •
>
> The current lifetime exclusion is the equivalent of $600,000 for each person that may be transferred free of estate taxes. The amount that can be given to a spouse is unlimited.

The tax consequences of poor planning can be enormous. Anything over $600,000 left in a parent's estate—$1.2 million for a couple properly planning their estate—is subject to federal, state, and local death taxes that can add up to a rate as high as 60%.

Don't lapse into fiscal irresponsibility before your parents die, simply because you're counting on a windfall to bail you out. What sounds like a big inheritance can vanish quickly—whether in a stock-market plunge, in medical bills, or nursing home expenses. To neglect your own retirement saving or assume that your parents' money will educate your children is a real gamble.

Naming Your Beneficiaries

Tips for Future Heirs
• • • • • • • • • • • • • • • •

- If your parents have not brought up the subject themselves, tactfully ask them to involve you in their estate planning. Talk to your children, too.
- Don't abandon your current program of saving and investing because you're counting on a windfall later.
- Get to know the family lawyer, accountant, and money manager. Will you be comfortable working with your parents' advisers?
- Be sure your parents understand the benefits of making cash gifts during their lifetime: Each parent can give up to $10,000 a year per person tax-free.
- If you have children, consider putting part of your inheritance in trust as a safeguard for their future.

There are certain assets you own that require naming a beneficiary. They may include: contracts for life insurance, annuities, IRAs and other retirement accounts. These accounts may represent the greatest amount available to you during retirement or to your family after your death.

The beneficiary will become the new owner of the proceeds of your account at your death. Because they may represent such a major part of your net worth, it is important how you name your beneficiaries.

Normally a husband and wife will name each other as the primary beneficiary, and their children will be the contingent beneficiaries equally of the accounts. The contingent beneficiaries will only receive the benefit if the primary beneficiary is not living when a benefit becomes payable. However, this may all be complicated by divorce or disability.

Children may become the beneficiaries of a windfall before they are capable of making good decisions. A trust should be used as the beneficiary for minor children or where specific instructions are to be given to a trust manager or trustee.

Gifts to a charity are often made by naming the charity as the beneficiary. This can be done very simply by using a beneficiary designation.

Study Guide Questions

1. What happens if you die without a legal will?

2. What are the key considerations in the probate process?

3. What are the advantages and disadvantages of a living trust?

4. What factors should you consider in deciding whether to hold property in joint ownership?

5. What are some examples of assets which require the naming of a beneficiary?

6. What are some examples of annual gifts you can make to family members without paying any federal-gift tax?

7. When is a life insurance trust a wise estate planning technique?

8. Contrast living trusts and living wills.

9. What are the primary differences between outright charitable gifts, bequests, and charitable-remainder trusts?

10. Although you receive no income tax deduction, when should you consider a revocable charitable trust?

Step 10

"There is a time for everything, and a season for every activity under heaven."
Ecclesiastes 3:1

Strategies For
Life's Seasons

▶ Children and Teens: The Formative Years

▶ Your 20s and 30s: Establishing Your Firm Foundation

▶ Your 40s and 50s: The Peak Earning Years of Middle Age

▶ 60s Plus: The Retirement Years

▶ When You're Suddenly Single

A time to save, a time to spend. A time to take risks, a time to conserve. A time to face your own mortality. But when is the right time? Few of us have the discipline, foresight—or the need—to record our expenses every day, reallocate our investments as economic conditions change, or review our insurance coverage every few years. What usually jogs us into action is an event that changes our life: marriage, birth of a child, mid-life decisions, retirement, or death of a spouse.

What you do with your assets at age 40 should be different from what you will do with them at age 65. Your insurance needs will be different and your needs for estate planning vehicles will be different.

While your children are at home, your needs to provide income replacement for your family will be greater than at retirement—after you have built up assets that will generate income for retirement.

These stages of life dictate how you plan and what tools you may decide to use. The amount of assets at your disposal will also determine some of your planning.

Your estate planning will also be different if you have a "mixed" family with children from different marriages. There are many factors that will determine how you will plan for the future.

At any age, don't rely on your employer—if you have one—to take care of you. Corporate contributions to retirement savings plans are falling, old-fashioned pension plans are disappearing, and the trend is not likely to reverse itself.

How you plan at the various stages of life depends on a variety of factors. You are unique with your own unique dreams, plans, and objectives. The techniques you use in planning will vary with your understanding and use of the different tools. There are no absolutely right and wrong answers. When managing your money, learn to act your age!

"If we had no Winter, the Spring would not be so pleasant: if we did not sometimes taste of adversity, prosperity would not be so welcome."
Anne Bradstreet
1664

Children and Teens: The Formative Years

Talking about money can begin very early. Children as young as two or three show curiosity about the way the world works. We need to convey in a warm, simple, and loving way that the subject of money is important.

The values we teach kids about money can establish guidelines for a lifetime of handling their income in a confident manner. Kids learn money-smart skills by taking one small step at a time. Here are lessons you can apply to each age group.

What to Teach Children Ages 3 to 5 About Money

- To identify small coins and dollar bills by their correct names
- To keep money in a safe place
- To know how many cents each coin is worth
- When we spend money, it is gone
- We can't buy everything, so we make choices
- To start managing a small allowance
- To pay a 10% tithe of their allowance
- To divide allowance between giving, spending, and sharing banks
- To know where money comes from (usually work)
- Banks help keep our money safe until we need it
- Writing a check takes our money out of the bank

What to Teach Children Ages 6 to 8 About Money

- To identify bills and coins of larger denominations
- To count larger amounts of mixed coins
- To make change
- *That there is a difference between wants and needs*
- To experience spending money
- To read price tags and look for things on sale
- To match appropriate amounts of money with things to buy
- To be sure correct change is given for a purchase

- To save toward a short-term goal (no longer than 1 month)
- To measure the promises of advertisements
- To prioritize expenses
- To realize that money can be earned by doing extra jobs
- To deposit money in a saving account

What to Teach Children Ages 9 to 12 About Money

- To make a daily diary for expenditures
- To make a simple spending plan for the week
- To apply the 10% tithe to money that is earned in addition to money received as an allowance
- To compare prices when shopping
- To cooperate with family efforts to save on utilities
- To look for ways to earn extra money for special goals
- To save a small amount each week for a large expense
- To be comfortable asking questions when considering a purchase
- To look at the value, not just the cost, of products
- To understand how parents use their checkbooks
- To understand the principle of compound interest
- To understand and use correct terms for banking transactions
- To learn how economic realities affect your family

What to Teach Children Ages 13 to 18 About Money

- To understand the value of wise investing in stocks, bonds, mutual funds, and collectibles
- To make a hypothetical portfolio and follow some stocks
- To look at the financial page for news about familiar companies
- To understand jargon such as *shares*, *dividends*, *mutual funds*, *risk*, *reward*, *prospectus*, *commission*, *bid*, and *asked*
- To keep financial records

How Kids Can Earn Money ● ● ● ● ● ● ● ● ●

The key is teaching kids to (1) recognize opportunities to make money, (2) work hard, and (3) become financially independent early. These are just a few examples of money-making opportunities:

- Babysitting
- Typing/ wordprocessing
- Pet and plant sitting
- House-sitting
- Lawn mowing
- Garage cleaning
- Running errands
- Gift wrapping
- Tutoring
- Golf caddying
- Window washing
- Helping people move (packing, cleaning up)

- To purchase independently of parents
- To understand the benefits of having a job, including independence
- To consider taking at-home work experiences into the neighborhood
- To manage a job without its interfering with schoolwork
- To read warranties and understand them
- To become an educated consumer about any major purchase
- To recognize the need for credit and how to use it responsibly
- To establish credit
- To understand what is meant by credit history, collateral, finance charges, service charges, APR, and installment credit
- To open a checking account and learn to balance the checkbook
- To use money machines and check-guarantee cards with moderation and keep track of transactions

Your 20s and 30s: Establishing Your Firm Foundation

- **Buy a home.** This could be your single largest investment, especially if you buy a single-family home rather than a condominium. Purchasing a home can get your housing costs under control, obtain tax breaks by itemizing deductions, and start building wealth.
- **Start an emergency fund.** Sock away at least three months' expenses. The money is a cushion against unexpected jolts. Use it only for genuine emergencies—not ski trips.
- **Start investing now.** You've got to start somewhere. Investing just $100 a month or $2,000 a year in an IRA may not seem like a lot. But if you start putting away that sort of money when you're in your 20s or early 30s, it will make a huge difference at retirement. You may not have much money in your 20s. But you have one big

advantage: time.

- **Take advantage of company benefit plans.** Enrolling in a 401(k), 403(b), or 457 retirement savings plan and making contributions of even as little as $50 a month can make a big difference quickly. If you're worried about "locking the money up" until retirement, consider this: Most plans allow you to borrow as much as 50% of the account balance and pay yourself back. So the money will be there if you need help with the down payment on a home or for children's college education expenses.

  Use a dependent-care reimbursement account. This can help you pay for child-care or elder-care expenses and can get you a tax break as well. A medical-care reimbursement account will do the same for doctor and hospital bills not picked up by your insurance.

> ## Tip for New Parents
> • • • • • • • • • • • • • • • • •
>
> Be sure to add the baby to your health coverage. You usually have 30 days from the date of birth to do it without proving medical insurability.

- **Protect yourself.** Make sure you have comprehensive insurance coverage. You may be tempted to go without insurance because you don't think you have much to protect. A gap in your insurance can wipe out years of savings and future earnings. Disability and umbrella liability insurance are often neglected.

  Buy life insurance, especially if you've acquired a house and you are a new parent. You'll want to provide enough for your surviving spouse to continue making mortgage payments or to pay off the loan, and meet other household expenses. Buy coverage equal to 15 times your annual living expenses, plus an extra chunk for the college fund. Because you'll need a lot of coverage, your budget will probably be strained. Term insurance is likely your best buy.

- **Control your debt.** Be sure that interest isn't working against you. Pay off those credit-card debts. Limit yourself to one credit card. Never

Disability Income Insurance Is Critical · · · · · · · · · · · · · · · ·

The greatest asset you have is your income. The disability-income coverage through your employer may not be adequate. Consider a private policy to supplement your employer's coverage.

let the outstanding balance exceed four weeks' net pay. You are establishing a credit history, which means that it's important to pay your bills on time.

When going for that first mortgage, finance no more than 80% of the purchase price if at all possible. The interest rate is likely to be a little lower, and you probably won't have to pay extra for mortgage insurance.

Family members may be willing to help out with a loan for the down payment. But, if you do borrow from Mom or Dad or other relatives, treat it as a business transaction. Be aware that borrowing from your family often causes family disharmony.

- **Check your beneficiaries.** Change your beneficiary. If you have a pension plan or a life insurance policy through your employer, remember to change the beneficiary from your parents to your spouse.

  Name your child or your trust as a contingent beneficiary on any group life-insurance or pension plan.

- **Save, save, save.** If your children are still young, you can stick with growth-oriented investments. But if you have teenagers, lean more

Investing for Long-Term Growth °

With young families to provide for, many investors in this age group prefer to reduce their portfolios' risk level. Don't overdo it, though. Those in their 20s and 30s should put 70% to 80% of their long-term investment money into stocks and/or stock mutual funds. The remainder should go into bonds or bond funds.

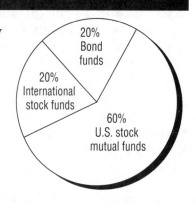

20% Bond funds

20% International stock funds

60% U.S. stock mutual funds

heavily on safer instruments.

To keep your sanity, try to save at least half the amount your child will need for college. When the time comes, you may be able to use your salary, a home equity loan, or your child's own earnings or savings to make up the difference.

Savings-Smart Tip

Whether you are twentysomething or sixtysomething, it's never too late to establish savings habits that will stay with you for the rest of your life.

- **Plan now if you want to retire early.** Almost half of all working-age people hope to retire before age 65. Some do it—but they actually can't afford to. Today, only 7% of people reaching age 65 are financially independent, in this the wealthiest country in the world.

  Successful early retirees typically established that goal in their 20s and 30s, when they still had plenty of time to accumulate wealth. They sacrificed early by saving 10% or 15% of their income and living in cheaper housing than they could afford.

- **Estate planning.** For a newly married couple with few assets, a will may not be critical, but it is prudent. You'll also want to decide whether to take joint title to things you acquire together. At this stage, joint ownership makes sense for assets such as your cars, house, and bank accounts.

  Have a durable power-of-attorney prepared, naming your spouse to act as your agent should you become incapacitated.

  Name a guardian. Both of you need wills to name a guardian for your children and to distribute assets you've acquired.

Your 40s and 50s: The Peak Earning Years of Middle Age

You just turned 40. All of a sudden college and retirement—events that used to seem about as relevant as which team would win the Super Bowl in the year 2000, are looming on the not-so-distant horizon.

What if you have never really done any conscious planning and in your 40s or 50s you realize that it's now or never? Far from being an exception, you are in the majority. At 40, it's time to get really serious about financial planning.

- **Consider your gift programs—both charitable and personal.** This is the season of life to begin making significant gifts to your church or charity through charitable-remainder trusts. You may also want to take full advantage of the $10,000 annual gift-tax exclusion or $20,000 if a spouse joins in the gift to individuals.

- **Adjust your insurance.** Upgrade your homeowners policy. Make sure your house is insured for its full replacement cost. Umbrella liability coverage is a must. It's at this point in life that you may be involved in community groups, and that may increase your exposure.

  After you hit age 40, the premiums on term life insurance begin to rise rapidly. Depending on the age of your children, you may be able to cut back on coverage. If you still need coverage, consider a cash-value or lifetime level-term policy. Don't automatically "convert" your term policy to a cash-value plan from the same insurer. If you are in good health, you may find a better deal or more attractive policy elsewhere.

  Have enough life insurance to cover your mortgage and kids' college education, and to provide a big enough nest egg so that your family can live comfortably off the earnings.

  Consider long-term-care insurance. At age 50, premiums are substantially cheaper. If you wait until age 60 or later, you risk not being healthy enough to obtain the coverage.

- **Reduce your debt.** These are usually your peak earning years—a good time to start reducing your debt burden in preparation for retirement. Having a lot of debt is riskier now than when you were in

"A man's treatment of money is one of the most decisive tests of his character, how he makes it and how he spends it."
James Moffett

your 20s. The potential for serious illness is greater, and middle-age professionals who are laid off often have a hard time finding another job.

Think carefully before borrowing against the equity in your home to start a business, or to invest in someone else's business. Consider your ability to service that loan over its term if the business fails.

Borrowing against a cash-value life insurance policy can provide easy access to money at comparatively low rates. But pay it back quickly or you've diminished the value of the policy for your survivors.

- **Minimize taxes.** Make full use of tax-deferred savings vehicles, including 401(k) plans, Individual Retirement Accounts (IRAs), and variable annuities. Your 40s and 50s are your peak earning years and, hence, your peak tax years, so tax-favored savings are important.
- **Project your retirement income and expenses.** Do this once a year, so you know how much you

Invest for Growth and Diversify

You should have 60% to 80% of your investment portfolio in stocks or stock mutual funds and the remainder in bonds. When you're within 10 years of retirement, you may be tempted to cash in your stocks and tuck the proceeds into bond funds or CDs. But at age 55, you may have a lifetime of 25 years ahead of you. Keep that same mix but change the types of securities you own to reduce your risk. Put less money into growth mutual funds and more into growth-and-income funds. Opt for higher-quality bond funds instead of high-yield junk-bond funds. Utility funds are also an option.

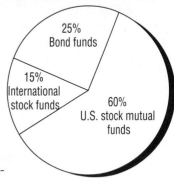

Diversify, diversify, diversify. Make sure all your funds are invested in at least five to seven different equity opportunities ranging from value funds to international funds.

After you have contributed the maximum to your 401(k), 403(b), 457 plan, or IRA, consider putting money in a low-cost tax-deferred variable annuity. Plan to stick with it for 10 years or so because of the high fees.

need to be saving and when you can retire. And don't forget to consider inflation of approximately 5.9% a year (the average rate over the last 20 years). By the time you're in your 50s, you can get a pretty good fix on what Social Security and your company pension will pay you. The real question is how much savings you'll have—and whether you need to save a lot more.

- **Plan your estate.** Everyone in their 40s and 50s should have three basic estate-planning documents—a will, a durable power of attorney or living trust (in case you become incapacitated), and a living will with a health care proxy.

    Your estate may be within shouting distance of the ceiling on assets that escape federal estate taxes—$600,000 for each spouse—if you own a house that has appreciated in value, as well as insurance policies, a company retirement plan, and other personal assets. If so, you need to meet with an attorney or financial adviser about more advanced strategies, such as testamentary trusts and life insurance trusts. A lot of people mistakenly believe that they aren't rich enough for these very effective estate-tax savings strategies.

60s Plus: The Retirement Years

Your focus should be on what you will do after age 65. Do you want to take early retirement? Work to the traditional age of 65? Is there an option to continue working, either full- or part-time?

If you are struggling to save enough money for retirement, consider staying in the workforce longer. There's tremendous financial leverage from delaying your retirement. (There are often physical and emotional benefits to continuing to work at least part-time.) If you delay your retirement from age 62 to 65, it can change the amount of capital you will need dramatically.

Expected expenses in the retirement years should be estimated. Of course, there will be inflation before and during retirement.

Deciding where you will reside in retirement is very important. Living expenses can often be reduced by selling a larger home in the suburbs and moving to a home or condo in a retirement area.

- **Keep saving.** A $2,000 monthly pension may look pretty good now. But with a 5% inflation rate, in 15 years, $2,000 will only have the purchasing power of $1,000. Rather than spending all of their investment gains, retirees under age 75 should continue to reinvest some of their gains so that the inflation-adjusted value of their savings doesn't decline.

- **Insurance and benefits.** Rethink your coverage. You may no longer need life insurance. But if you have an estate large enough to trigger estate taxes, consider holding on to a policy that could be used to pay taxes and cover the administrative expenses of settling the estate.

  You may need additional coverage to pay estate taxes. "Second-to-die" coverage that pays only when both the husband and wife have died should be considered. But you don't need insurance to pay estate taxes if you hold sufficient marketable securities outside your retirement plan that could be easily sold. Through your charitable generosity, you can reduce the potential estate-tax burden with charitable remainder trusts.

  If you don't need the money, it generally makes sense to hang on to an older cash-value policy. You could face a big income-tax bill on the investment gains within

The Litmus Test of Your Planning

• • • • • • • • • • • • • • • •

- Will the Lord say "Well done thou good and faithful servant"?
- As an accountable steward-manager, how would you want to be judged?
- Will your family regret the type of planning you have already done?
- Will you be remembered as one who died the way he lived?
- Will your planning cause division in your family?

the policy if you drop the coverage now. In contrast, if you hold the policy to death, all the investment gains escape income tax. Consider converting to "paid-up" status, which would trim the death benefit some but eliminate the need to pay further premiums.

A protracted illness is the biggest out-of-pocket risk you face. The retirement equivalent of disability insurance is long-term-care insurance. Anyone over age 50 with assets between $200,000 and $1 million should consider this coverage.

Health insurance is also a concern, especially if you or your spouse is under 65 and not eligible for Medicare. Your employer may provide coverage. If not, federal law requires most employers to allow you and your spouse to continue in the company's group plan for 18 months following retirement. After that, you may have the option to convert to an individual policy.

- **Try to be debt-free.** In the best of all possible worlds, you would be debt-free as you enter retirement. But it isn't unusual for people in their 60s and 70s to have home mortgages and car loans.

  Some things don't change when you're older. You still have to consider your cash flow and the cost of the debt. Fixed-rate loans generally are better than variable rates and shorter-term debt is preferable to long-term debt.

  If you have the equity and need the cash but you wouldn't qualify for standard borrowing, you might consider a "reverse mortgage." This is a loan based on the equity a homeowner has accumulated and usually disbursed in monthly installments over a period of years. But these loans can be costly.

- **Taxes.** Retirement triggers a new round of tax issues. For example, if you're eligible for a lump-sum retirement distribution, your best bet probably is to roll it into an IRA, where your money will continue to earn tax-deferred interest. As long as you're over age $59^1/2$, you can begin taking money out of the account without penalty as you need it.

If you take the lump sum in cash, you'll owe income tax on the full amount, but if you need the bulk of the money fairly soon after retiring, forward-averaging over five or ten years may ease the bite.

- **Review estate plans every few years.** You may want to change the beneficiaries in your will if, for example, there's a divorce—or death in the family or if there is a grandchild who has special needs.

Selling Your Home ●●●●●●●●●●●●●●●●

Don't forget the special tax break on the sale of your home. After you reach age 55, you may qualify to pocket tax-free $125,000 in profit from the sale of your home.

Investing for Growth and Income

The biggest mistake you can make in retirement is to radically change the way you invest. At 65, the joint remaining life expectancy of a married male and female is 22 years. Be flexible because the health of you or your spouse could change dramatically. You may have to dip into principal to meet your needs. This requires a portfolio like the one shown in the top chart. Keep at least 40% of your money in growth and income or utility stocks (or in mutual funds that hold such issues).

After you turn 75, portfolio growth is less important, and you can safely cut back your equity holding to 30% or less, as shown in the lower chart. *The reason:* Your reduced life expectancy makes inflation less of a threat. By boosting the amount you keep in cash and bonds or bond mutual funds and putting half of your remaining stock investments into high-yield issues of income-oriented funds, you should raise your yield while still keeping sufficient inflation protection to maintain your standard of living for the rest of your life.

Early Retirement

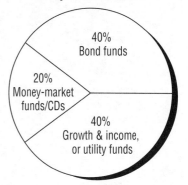

40% Bond funds

20% Money-market funds/CDs

40% Growth & income, or utility funds

Late Retirement

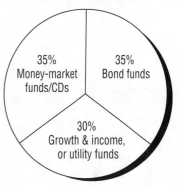

35% Money-market funds/CDs

35% Bond funds

30% Growth & income, or utility funds

Investment and Estate Planning For A Lifetime

	AGE UNDER 40	AGE 40-59	AGE 60 PLUS
HOME	Start early. Consider as lifestyle not investment.	same	Consider taking capital-gains tax exclusion if moving to a smaller home.
COLLEGE	Begin saving early.	Pay from current income/loans.	Gifts to grandchildren for tuition.
EMERGENCY FUND	Savings accounts and 401(k), 403(b), or 457 plans. Plan to have 3 to 6 months cost-of-living fund for emergencies.	Savings accounts, Life insurance cash values and 401(k), 403(b), or 457 accounts.	Retirement accounts and savings accounts. Have some funds readily accessible for emergencies.
RETIREMENT	Start saving early. Save regularly and as automatically as possible. Use growth long-term investments.	Maximize savings. Invest for long-term growth. Allocate to various asset classifications for diversification.	Must begin withdrawals at 70 1/2 based on life expectancy. Invest for growth and income. Allocate to various asset classifications for diversification.
ADVISORS YOU MAY NEED	Financial Adviser Accountant Attorney Insurance Agent	Financial Adviser Accountant Attorney Insurance Agent	Financial Adviser Accountant Attorney Insurance Agent Trustee
WILLS, TRUSTS, AND ESTATE PLANNING	Use Wills, Testamentary trusts, UGMA accounts, Joint accounts.	Living trusts and Joint spousal accounts. Consider a Living Will.	Use all of the following that apply to you: Gifts to family Living Trusts Family Trusts Charitable Trusts Life-Insurance Trusts Living Will

Insurance Planning For A Lifetime

	UNDER 40	40-59	60 PLUS
LIFE	Low-cost term or universal life Buy as much coverage as you can afford.	Low-cost term universal life or whole life Get rid of any unnecessary insurance.	Universal life, whole life or last-survivor life Consider loans or other ways to use your cash values to enhance your retirement income.
AUTO AND LIABILITY	Make sure your liability coverage is at least $300,000. Drop collision coverage on older autos.	Add umbrella coverage to increase liability coverage to at least $1,000,000. Drop collision coverage on older autos.	Review your liability coverage. Increase if necessary. Drop collision coverage on older autos.
HOMEOWNERS	Buy replacement coverage along with liability protection. Raise the deductibles to lower your premiums.	Add umbrella coverage to increase liability protection. Add endorsements or floaters to protect valuables, such as antiques and jewelry.	Make sure policy will cover rebuilding and refurnishing your home. Review liability coverage, endorsements, and floaters.
DISABILITY INCOME	Review coverage through your job. If necessary, add supplemental coverage with your own policy.	Review your coverage for adequacy.	Drop your coverage when you retire.
MEDICARE SUPPLEMENT	Not needed until retirement.	Not needed until retirement.	Consider your ability to self-insure. If you have limited resources, you should consider coverage to supplement Medicare.
LONG-TERM CARE	Generally not available until later. Consider for your parents.	Consider purchase of this coverage while you are healthy. Consider your parents' need for this coverage.	You should purchase coverage that will protect your assets from being spent on nursing-care costs.

Investment Tip For Seniors
• • • • • • • • • • • • • • • • •

Because scam artists frequently prey on the elderly, seniors should always check with someone they trust before making major financial decisions.

If you haven't already drafted a durable power of attorney, giving an agent you name authority to handle your financial affairs if you can't, do it now. If you want a more flexible alternative that lets you plan for the future handling of your assets, consider a revocable living trust (see page 209).

- **Keep loved ones informed.** You should talk to family members about your finances, health care arrangements, insurance, and what should happen if you can no longer care for yourself. If necessary, children should initiate these discussions with their parents.

When You're Suddenly Single

You have been married but suddenly you are single. You may never have handled all of the family finances. What do you do now?

The best advice is—wait to act. You need time—time to carefully consider your financial affairs. Just learning to manage money on a day-to-day basis can be a challenge.

You may have more money than you've ever had to deal with. You'll be besieged by people who want you to buy or sell something. Your best response is to say no.

Find a good financial adviser. Ask your friends for recommendations for someone you can trust.

Estate planning. Revising your will is essential and should be one of your first priorities. You'll need to change the beneficiaries on your insurance policy. Also, a big settlement from insurance on your spouse's life could boost your estate significantly. If you haven't already drafted a durable power of attorney or considered a revocable living trust, do it now. If you have young children, review their guardians and decide whether you want to set up trusts on their behalf.

Taxes. Take a break on the appreciation of your property. The tax on any appreciation in the value of property owned by your spouse—whether it's a house or a mutual fund—is forgiven when he or she dies. If you owned property jointly, there is no tax on half of the profit.

Even if your spouse's estate escapes the federal estate tax, there may be state inheritance taxes. You don't owe income tax on life insurance proceeds. You can file a joint return for the year of your spouse's death, and you can use joint-return rates for two years after the death if you have a child who qualifies as a dependent.

Insurance and benefits. Decide what to continue. You may be able to drop your life insurance altogether. However, if you have young children, you may need to beef up life and disability protection. If your health insurance was covered by your spouse's policy, group coverage for you and your children must continue for 36 months under most policies (although you may be required to pay up to 102% of the premium). After that, you may be able to convert to an individual policy from the employer's group plan or get coverage elsewhere.

Social Security. You may be entitled to the full benefit of your spouse, adjusted for the age you begin receiving benefits.

Study Guide Questions

1. Highlight some basic differences in financial planning for the different seasons of life.

2. List several ways to teach your children the value of money.

3. What are some of the ways your life-insurance needs will change as you get older?

4. How will your investment strategies change at different ages?

5. What are some ways your savings patterns may change over your life span?

6. What concerns might you have about your personal debt at various stages of life?

7. How do your retirement strategies change based on the seasons of life?

8. What charitable-giving vehicles should you consider at different ages?

9. As you grow older, how do your estate planning needs change?

10. What are some of your financial concerns if you're suddenly single?

THE BOTTOM LINE . . .

The management of our resources isn't nearly as important as the destiny of our souls. Since we are born to have fellowship with an eternal God, our eternal destiny is the ultimate "bottom line." God's Word not only promises us a quality of life on earth—as we utilize His plan and faithfully manage what He has loaned to us—it also gives us a hope for the future. *"I write these things to you who believe in the name of the Son of God so that you may know that you have eternal life" (1 John 5:13).*

If you carefully consider every other principle of this book and neglect the one that links them all, then the authors have come short of their goal. God promises life beyond the grave to those who have transferred their spiritual trust from self to the Lord Jesus Christ. How do you make this transfer (if you haven't already)?

- Acknowledge sin in your life and determine to turn from that sin *(Romans 3:23).*

- Believe that God's solution for sin is personal faith in His Son, the Lord Jesus Christ and receive God's forgiveness *(Romans 6:23).*

- Invite the Lord Jesus Christ into your life in prayer *(Revelation 3:20).*

- Make a public declaration of your personal decision to repent of sin and follow the Lord Jesus Christ *(Matthew 10:32).*

- Stand on the authority of God's Word that your past is forgiven and your future is secure as you walk in obedience to the Lord Jesus Christ *(1 John 1:9).*